Jan-Michael Vincent

Edge of Greatness

By David Grove

Jan-Michael Vincent: Edge of Greatness
© 2016. David Grove All rights reserved.

All illustrations are copyright of their respective owners, and are also reproduced here in the spirit of publicity. Whilst we have made every effort to acknowledge specific credits whenever possible, we apologize for any omissions, and will undertake every effort to make any appropriate changes in future editions of this book if necessary.

No part of this book may be reproduced in any form or by any means, electronic, mechanical, digital, photocopying or recording, except for the inclusion in a review, without permission in writing from the publisher.

Published in the USA by:
BearManor Media
P O Box 71426
Albany, Georgia 31708
www.bearmanormedia.com

Printed in the United States of America
ISBN   978-1-62933-084-6 (paperback)

Book & cover design and layout by Darlene Swanson • www.van-garde.com

Contents

Part One	Hanford Kid, 1944-1966	1
Part Two	Stand and Deliver, 1967-1973	35
Part Three	Easy to Steer, 1974-1983	89
Part Four	The Defiant One, 1984-1994	149
Part Five	The One Take Wonder, 1995-2017	175
	Filmography	193
	Bibliography	209
	Acknowledgments	211
	Index	213

Part One

Hanford Kid

1944-1966

"I made it tough for myself."

1
Not a Simple Life

The old man is lonely, which is not the same as alone. He lives with a woman who takes care of him. He calls her his wife.

He still has his surfboard, and when he closes his eyes and listens to the waterfalls embedded in the wooded hills, and the soft ripple from the nearby lake, he sometimes finds himself transported back to Malibu, but there are no beaches here, and there are no waves, except during the flash floods. He has a prosthetic right leg and is confined to a wheelchair.

He lives in Eagle Lake, Mississippi, in a neglected house overlooking the base of the Delta—the bayous and swamps, and the vast encampment of rusted trailers, one of which he used to live in. A black Mustang convertible and a patch of roses out front offer the only clues to his past life, when his aquamarine eyes, chiseled features, and sun-streaked hair sang of creamy sand and sweet sex.

He has long ceased to be beautiful or strong: there is brain damage; a 2012 amputation, the result of complications from peripheral artery disease, took most of his right leg; he struggles with diabetes and epilepsy; he barely weighs 100 pounds; his teeth dangle in his jaw, brittle and emaciated.

Despite countless episodes of alcoholic poisoning and toxic shock, he has never undergone a liver transplant. It miraculously endures, lodged under his ribs, like a brown, fatty tumor, a grisly tableau of the once seemingly inexhaustible well of vitality he plundered through. Its condition has moved far beyond the simple characterization of cirrhosis. It is a celebration of rot.

Her name is Anna, and she was once a very beautiful woman, before she assumed the role of caregiver. Getting him up every morning is a major operation: he has to be gingerly bathed and changed; the socket and stump have to be constantly monitored, antiseptically, for infection. Then he can be dressed.

She chauffeurs him around in the convertible. He has no one else.

Gifts were bestowed upon him. Even his ordinary height—he was five ten when he could still stand in his shoes—was ideal in terms of establishing a relationship with the camera, which is not the same as acting.

He had no use for the tools he was given; there was not a speck of desire implanted in him. He only wanted to be a surfer.

His obituary could've been written thirty years ago, when he was in his early forties, and then kept on file, which is what media outlets do when a celebrity or public figure enters their seventies, when they are marked for death. His age, location, and the year—these are the only new details that need to be filled in.

> Jan-Michael Vincent, a film and television actor, whose career and personal life descended into a nightmare of alcohol and drug abuse.

They will condense the previous thirty years into the tragic event that put him into a wheelchair and led him to Mississippi: the 1996 car crash that left him with three broken vertebrae in his neck and a crushed voice box. Jan wrote a short poem.

> There's so much about it I don't remember
> So I guess I'll go ahead and take the blame
> I went and lost my mind to some beer and wine
>
> Yes, I went temporarily insane
> I went God knows where
> With good old what's her name

As an actor, he is most commonly remembered for *Airwolf*, the television series he starred in from 1984 to 1986, which isn't the same as being conscious.

That was a period in which he still appeared, on camera at least, lithe and trim, even as those around him started asking him the question: Why are you doing this to yourself? His reply, back then, took the form of a self-eulogy.

> I'm a drunk. I've been a drunk all my life, and
> I always will be.

They will mention all of the Hollywood legends he was paired with in his career—from John Wayne to Robert Mitchum to Burt Reynolds, and many more. He'd starred in many feature films, but he was not a movie star.

He was, on and off screen, a man of few words, who found it difficult to describe what happened, though he did try.

> An actor's life for me—tweedly-deedly-dee
> An actor's life is fun—tweedly-deedly-dum
> You can wear your hair in a pompadour
> and ride around in a coach and four
> and drop on by at a candy store
> An actor's life for me

There are contradictions to be found throughout his career and life: he was a teen idol in his late twenties, part actor, part male model; he was a matinee idol who desperately sought a wider range; he always looked at least ten years younger than he was; he was still playing the role of teenager when he was a husband and father.

He finally looks his age.

2
Small Town Boy

He was just Jan.

No one had ever heard of Michael, until he left the tiny world he grew up in, and no one spoke of Jasper, which was the original name his parents had chosen for their firstborn child.

Jan was born on July 15, 1944, in Denver, Colorado, where his father, Lloyd Whiteley Vincent (September 7, 1919—August 30, 2000), who was a B-25 bomber pilot during World War II, was stationed after enlisting in the Army in 1941. Lloyd was born in Tulare, California but raised in nearby Hanford, a dull farming town in the San Joaquin Valley.

 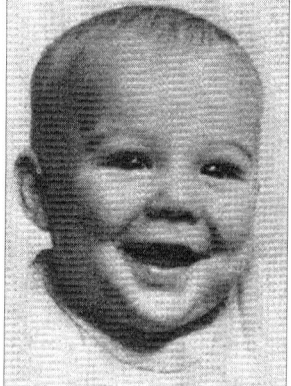

Left: **Jan, four months.** *Right:* **Jan, six months.**

It was in Denver, in the army, where Jan's rebellious persona—the persona that defined his adolescence and much of his screen career—was born, his mistrust of authority first established by seeing his father being manipulated by the rigid army system, being told what to do and when to do it, a system in which, from Jan's point-of-view, the individual was powerless—and a sucker. It was the same system in which Jan found himself trapped two decades later, the last common link between Jan and his father.

Jan's mother, Doris Jane Pace Vincent (August 2, 1925—February 22, 1993), was born in Arkansas and relocated to Hanford when she was a toddler, after her mother left Doris' father and remarried. In 1940, Doris was in her early teens and a student at Hanford High when she met Lloyd, who had already graduated, and they soon started dating secretly. Doris then followed Lloyd to Denver, when he was transferred there in March 1941, and they got married the following year, eloping in Las Vegas when Doris was sixteen. Jan's sister, Jaqueline "Jacquie" Vincent, was born in 1947, and she was followed by Jan's brother, Christopher, who was born in 1952.

Jan's body type and slow-developing beauty was inherited not from Doris but from Lloyd, who was a handsome man; Lloyd was trim, with blonde-streaked hair, though the resemblance between Christopher and Lloyd, who appear now as twins when compared alongside each other at matching ages, turned out to be far more striking than that of Jan and Lloyd as Christopher got older.

Doris was a plain-featured but shapely woman, who later—after the family's fortunes brightened in Hanford—made herself look beautiful by coloring her hair, wearing her hair up, sometimes in a French twist, which accentuated her figure, which was always held in high regard, especially from behind.

Lloyd became a painter like his father—Jan's grandfather, Herbert Vincent (September 26, 1876—January 14, 1974), who was also, much more prosperously, a notorious criminal, a bank robber and counterfeiter, who masterminded several armed robberies in the 1920s and 1930s, most of which took place in Hanford's surrounding counties, though, in 1924, Hoy Vincent, the eldest of Herbert's five sons, was shot to death in Tulare by a Sheriff's deputy, who was attempting to arrest Hoy for a bank robbery that Hoy had executed in Oregon.

Herbert was a brutal, unforgiving man, who would sacrifice anyone and everything within his reach if he felt the slightest risk to himself, including his sons. In 1931, sons Clifford and Harold were convicted for robbing banks in Hardwick and Strathmore, which left son Gordon, Herbert's right hand man, and young Lloyd, who was only twelve in January of 1932, when Gordon and Herbert were arrested in Hanford, charged with bank robbery and assault with a deadly weapon with the intent to commit murder, after the Vincent Gang—Herbert, Gordon, and Herbert's son-in-law, Arthur Gordon—held up and robbed the First National bank in Caruthers, California, which yielded just over $4,000 for the trio. There was a shootout, a spectacular escape, and a chase.

Herbert, who also had two daughters, did not kill anyone, at least on record, which is the only reason why Herbert, who spent the rest of the 1930s in prison, was able to play such an active role in Jan's early life in the mid to late 1940s. He was a loving grandfather.

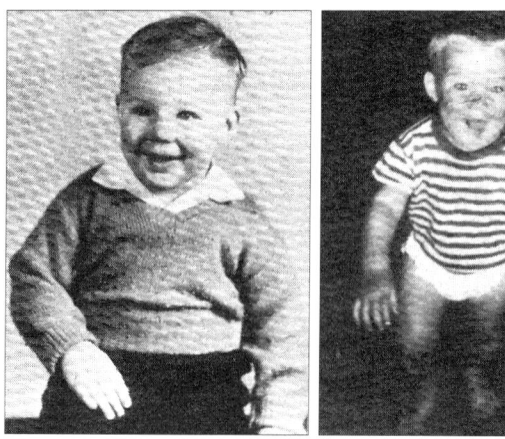

Left: Jan turns one. *Right:* Jan as a toddler

Although Lloyd avoided his family's criminal activities, entirely because of his age, he inherited Herbert's alcoholism, which was passed down to

Lloyd, and then to Jan, bypassing Jan's siblings, who both went on to lead happy, normal, productive lives: Christopher, who has raised a family, runs a construction business near Hanford, while Jacquie, who has also raised a family in California, spent many years working with the disabled.

Lloyd turned into a heavy drinker, mostly socially; his alcoholism did not inflict any serious damage on his career or his relationships, his drinking minor compared to that of Herbert, who lived, with Jan's grandmother, Harriet Whiteley Vincent (September 14, 1877—May 8, 1958), on a twenty acre farm on the outskirts of Hanford, where Jan—who was much closer to his grandfather than he was to Lloyd, before Jan and his family moved into their first house in Hanford—spent much of his early childhood, bonding with the plentiful supply of animals—he had a pet turtle, named Timothy, and was given a horse, Shadow, when he was six and still very much a nerdy looking boy, even without his horn rimmed glasses.

The Vincents were not a churchgoing family, and Jan wasn't baptized as a baby; his baptism took place in Grade eight, when his first girlfriend, Dianne Milliken, convinced him to join her confirmation class at the local Presbyterian church, where Jan was baptized in front of the congregation.

Hanford was a small town, more in spirit than geography, Hanford's total area covering more than sixteen square miles, Hanford's population remaining static at the 10,000 level throughout the 1950s.

Hanford looked like a town in the deep south in the 1950s, the 1960s never really beginning in Hanford until the Kennedy assassination in 1963, the year Jan graduated from Hanford High, the oldest member of the Class of 1963.

Hanford was segregated, blacks all but invisible, and cotton was the bedrock of the farming sector. It was a place where everyone knew everyone's business and the girls pretended to be virgins.

 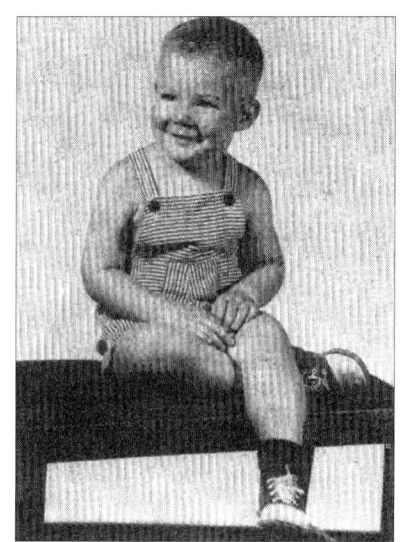

Left: **Jan at two.** *Right:* **Jan on his third birthday.**

Jan and his family moved, permanently, from Denver to Hanford in 1956; their first home in Hanford, outside of Herbert's farm, was a modest house on Amelia Avenue, a neighborhood in which all of the houses had been built in the early 1950s, the neighborhood comprised mostly of starter homes for young families.

Jan's bookish appearance, which was forever altered when he discarded his horn rimmed glasses for contact lenses in Grade eight, did not translate to academic success. Prior to Hanford High, Jan attended Roosevelt Elementary and Woodrow Wilson Junior High, Jan finding his greatest success at school, academically, in the subjects of Economics and History.

He struggled the most, and mightily so, with Math, and with Speech, the school subject most applicable to his later career—a career that was not at all chosen by him but rather for him. Although some of Jan's classmates now say they weren't surprised by his ultimate pursuit of fame, most were—and remain—completely shocked.

Part One: Hanford Kid 1944-1966

Jan (middle) in late 1947. (Photo courtesy of Dean Hale)

Doris and Lloyd were loving parents, which they showed in very different ways. The bond between Jan and his mother was very apparent, whereas Lloyd rarely displayed affection. The relationship between Jan and his father, between the former Army pilot and his disaffected loner son, unfolding, throughout Jan's adolescence, as predictably as this clichéd dynamic would suggest, with Lloyd, whose political views were left of center, constantly getting on Jan, who gave his parents little to be proud of throughout his childhood and high school.

Lloyd, who described himself as a painter in the occupation section of his army admittance form in 1941, supported the family as a sign painter; he opened his own sign painting business, Lloyd Vincent Signs, which was located on Ford Street, adjacent to the Swift Ice Cream factory, across from the railroad tracks, the lot formerly occupied by a JC Penney warehouse. It is now a gun range.

Jan (middle) in 1957. (Photo courtesy of Dean Hale)

Lloyd specialized in building and designing road and rest stop signs—the business, and Lloyd's focus, shifted over time toward outdoor work, Lloyd an avid outdoorsman. Lloyd Vincent Signs eventually became Lloyd Vincent Outdoor and then Vincent Outdoor Advertising, as Lloyd, who obtained several design patents, began building outdoor adventure structures, as well as painting monuments, his work prominently displayed in local parks.

The business was an immediate success, enabling Lloyd to move the family to North Douty Street, a more established neighborhood, in the spring of 1959. The house on North Douty was larger than the Amelia Avenue property, the house built in the 1930s, the front yard adorned with a lovely rose garden, which Lloyd, who carved the address and the family name into the front entrance, tore up and replaced with a lawn, much to the dismay of the former owners and the neighbors. The house—which sat on the corner, not too far from Sacred Heart Hospital—was just a regular home, nothing fancy, but the move from Amelia to North Douty, along with the growth of Lloyd's business, signaled that Doris and Lloyd were set to join the ranks of Hanford's most prominent citizens.

Left: Jan (front row, left) in 1953, with his sister, Jacquie, his parents, Doris and Lloyd, and baby brother Christopher. *Right:* Jan and Jacquie.

As Lloyd grew more prosperous, Doris transformed. She started coloring her hair, dressing fashionably, transforming from traditional stay-at-home wife to a woman who put on airs. Doris and Lloyd became fixtures within Hanford's fledgling country club set, entertaining and playing golf at the country club, Doris gregarious, Lloyd remaining soft-spoken, drinking heavily but never during work hours.

Although Jan later studied commercial art in college, he showed little artistic ability at the shop, where he worked part-time between 1960 and 1963, Jan's responsibilities at the shop mostly limited to installing signs and running menial errands for his father.

When Jan made a habit out of turning up the radio at the shop too loud, Lloyd confiscated the radio, Lloyd just as annoyed that Jan had started listening to rock 'n' roll in the shop, instead of Country & Western music, the only genre allowed in the Vincent household when Jan was growing up.

Another time, Lloyd sent Jan to the paint store in a brand new Ford truck Lloyd had purchased. As Jan was driving back to the shop, he spilled paint in the truck. Lloyd never entrusted him with the keys to the truck again.

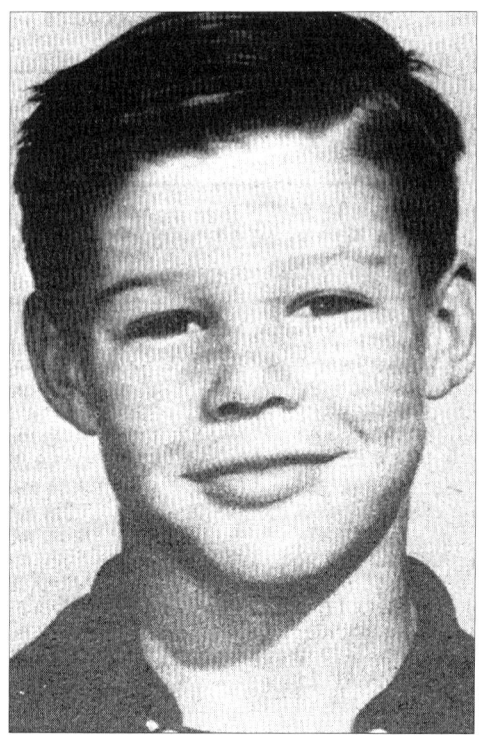

**Jan never invoked his middle name,
Michael, until he left Hanford.**

Jan was, in fact, fairly adept at basic painting and lettering, less so with drawing and sketching. He could've become a sign painter like Lloyd and taken over the business at some point, which was Jan's brother's destiny, not Jan's.

Some of Jan's former classmates, the ones who believe Jan was a born alcoholic, believe he would've ended up with the same problems had he stayed in Hanford and become a sign painter, a notion his small circle of friends disagree with.

He is at least a year older than the rest of the Hanford High Class of 1963; he missed a year of school between Denver and Hanford, because of the move, which left him stranded in Grade five, in no man's land. He was nearly nineteen when he graduated from high school.

None of the charisma that carried him through the early phase of his acting career was at all visible during his school years, and it wasn't until he abandoned the horn rimmed glasses that he received any interest from girls, most of whom considered him only so-so looking throughout junior high, far removed from the good-looking group. He was no Bobby Peters.

Jan's first serious girlfriend, Dianne Milliken, brought him out of his shell when they started dating at Woodrow Wilson Junior High in Grade eight. Dianne encouraged him to abandon the glasses and switch to contacts. She introduced him to her social group, and she convinced him to run for a position in the student government. He dropped out of the race before the election was held.

He was well known to local police but was never arrested. When he told his Hanford story in the 1970s, in celebrity interviews, he described himself as a punk growing up, admitting to having been his own worst enemy, mentioning drunkenness, fistfights, scrapes—exaggerating somewhat, for effect, claiming that he used to set off carbide bombs, which no one else remembers happening.

In the overall picture of a life that now seems more newsworthy than real, the most attention Jan received in his young life occurred in Grade eight, when Jan, without any explanation, ran away from home, from Hanford. His disappearance, which lasted three days, was big news in Hanford and was the beginning of everyone around him realizing that he was a rebel.

3
The Rebel Surfer

Jan attended Hanford High between 1959 and 1963, and this was a period when Jan, like Hanford and the rest of small town America, had one foot in the fifties and one foot in the sixties, caught between the *Happy Days* and *Leave it to Beaver* traditions of the 1950s and the turbulence of the sixties, as defined, in the pre-Kennedy assassination period, by the escalation of America's involvement in the Vietnam conflict, a subject Jan became very opinionated on, after graduating Hanford and leaving his hometown in the fall of 1963, when he underwent basic training in the National Guard between 1965 and 1966.

During his four years at Hanford High, the focus of Jan's estrangement narrowed while his social base expanded considerably. Hate is too strong of a word to describe Jan's feelings toward his teachers, but he never got along with any of them, or made an effort to. Jan, who was a good athlete but not a jock, tried out for the football team in Grade nine but quickly withdrew when he found the coach to be a sadistic drill sergeant who confused coaching with corporal punishment.

Jan with his girlfriend, Janet Odell, at the 1963
homecoming dance. (Photo courtesy of Leighton Gould)

He blossomed, physically, in Grade eleven, junior year, and he fell in love for the first time, with Janet Odell, a girl who was the complete opposite of him. Janet was the most popular girl at Hanford High, or one of them, and she belonged to every school club imaginable—all of the institutions that Jan avoided as if they were a plague.

As a couple, they were referred to as Jan and Jan at Hanford High and were nominated for Favorite Couple at the 1963 Homecoming Dance. Janet, like Doris, wasn't especially beautiful, but she possessed the same directness, energy, and forceful personality that Jan later found in his first wife, Bonnie, when they first met in 1964.

Janet was the most high profile girl at Hanford who took notice of Jan's emergence, but she wasn't the only one. He was, in his junior and senior year, considered passably handsome by an increasing number of girls at school but was still no match, in the looks department, for the best looking boy at Hanford High, Bobby Peters, who had dated Janet in junior high, which almost led to a fistfight between Bobby and Jan.

Teenage life in Hanford in the late fifties and early sixties didn't exactly mirror the film *American Graffiti* (1973), whose story is set in Modesto, California, in 1962. However, the rhythms and the teenage tribal rituals, on a typical Friday and Saturday night, were not that dissimilar from the film, which was largely shot, in 1972, in and around Petaluma, California, which is two square miles smaller, in total area, than Hanford and a nearly four hour drive from Hanford. The nearest Mel's Drive-In was in Visalia, twenty miles away.

The main teenage gathering spots in Hanford were the Me-N-Ed's pizza parlor on Main Street, where a lot of fights occurred, outside in the parking lot, and the Fosters Freeze, which was also located on Main Street and served burgers, milkshakes, and soft serve. There was also the Fox Theater, Hanford's movie theater; there was an A&W; there was a Superior Dairy ice cream parlor between Jan's house and the sign shop. Jan liked to burn rubber through Main Street in his 1956 Ford Lincoln, his first car, which he cherished, and took very good care of, as if it was a surfboard.

Jan's personal evolution began in December 1961, when the Beach Boys' first released single—"Surfin'"—began airing on California's most influential teen-oriented radio stations.

Jan, who loved the water and was a natural swimmer, fell in love with the Beach Boys and decided he wanted to be a surfer, which marked the beginning of what turned out to be the most committed, sustained relationship in his life.

In Grade twelve, senior year, Janet encouraged Jan to join the swimming team, another club she belonged to. He found comfort in the individual nature of competitive swimming, which, to him, represented the antithesis of the organized team sport structure he found so distasteful. He achieved good results, mostly in the short sprint distances, fifty and 100 yards, which made his girlfriend, and his parents, very happy.

Beyond Janet, and Lloyd's shop, Jan spent most of his free time with Frank Gonsalves, Monty Lee, and Charlie Oncea, three fellow students, all of whom shared the same aspiration: they wanted to become professional surfers. The foursome bought a car, a 1949 Ford Mercury wagon, which they owned and remodeled together, converting it into a Woodie Wagon, a surfing car.

Their surfing adventures took place on the weekends in junior and senior year, when they usually drove to Avila Beach and Pismo Beach, over 100 miles away from Hanford, sometimes going as far as Huntington, over 200 miles away. These weekend trips were, for Jan, a respite from his father, and from the intense pressure of standing alongside Janet. She was very liberal in her thinking but was also a self-directed person and did not approve of Jan's surfing.

If surfing began and ended for Jan, who continued surfing until the 1996 car crash, as a form of escapism, it never became a source of healing for him. His natural ability automatically made him a more than passable surfer but nothing more, the same pattern that developed after his introduction to acting—and then with marriage and fatherhood. He was a much better surfer in his late teens and early twenties than he was when he played a flawed but brilliant surfer in the film *Big Wednesday* (1978), when Jan was thirty-three and needed a surfing double.

Jan's surfing buddies enjoyed his company, and they had many good times together in their final two years of school. However, over time, his friends began to see the cavalier attitude and behavior that Lloyd tried to extinguish but was part of Jan's wiring and sometimes revealed itself, to his friends, as icy detachment.

They almost got arrested at Avila Beach, or two of Jan's friends did, when police officers approached the Woodie as underage Frank and Monty were drinking beer. Jan was walking back to the car when this was going on, alongside Charlie Oncea, the two of them returning from a nearby dance, and the company of girls, when they saw the police officers surround the car and their friends.

"They're going to arrest us," Charlie said.

"They're going to arrest them," Jan replied, pointing at the car, shaking his head.

On a chilly day at Pismo Beach in early 1963, Monty was a caught in a big wave and appeared to be in serious trouble. Jan was on the beach, watching, and when Charlie suggested they enter the freezing water to help Monty, Jan shrugged and said: "He can save himself."

Jan and his friends planned a dream surfing adventure in Mexico, during a three week window in the summer of 1963, after graduation. It never came to pass, due to parental interference, mostly from Lloyd.

They ended up selling their surfing car.

4
Stray Cat

Jan never gave any thought to becoming an actor before those around him, especially his father and girlfriend, saw the possibilities for him.

The first spark happened at the sign shop, one day in 1962, when a friend of Lloyd's—a salesman from Montroy Supply, a sign supplies distributor—made his regular visit to Lloyd's shop, took one look at Jan, and then told Jan and Lloyd that he knew a producer in Los Angeles, suggesting that Jan audition for the producer, for a television series the producer was doing. Lloyd, who was growing pessimistic about Jan's career prospects, was intrigued by the idea, which made Jan laugh out loud. Nothing happened with this, with a move toward acting, until late 1965, when Jan was in Los Angeles, on the verge of going to the Monterey Bay Peninsula in Central California to begin National Guard training at the Fort Ord army post.

```
                    CAST
    Dick Skinner  .........  Ray Morrow
    Tom Skinner   .......    Charles Oncea
    Harry Skinner ........   Phil Stearns
    Billy Jones   .........  Jim Casados
    Rev. Patterson .......   Jan Vincent
    Leona Brooks  .........  Janet Odell
    Wanda Taylor  ........   Toni Ricchetti
    Jennie Long   ..........  Janet Penny
    Kitty Baker   ..........  Janice Noga
```

**The introduction: the Hanford High production of *Stray Cats*.
(Photo courtesy of Leighton Gould)**

Janet was a member of Hanford High's Drama Club, which led to Jan joining the club in senior year, where he made little impression, serving as understudy to a student named Jon Rose, who recalls noticing Jan's handsomeness but otherwise had little interaction with Jan, who later spoke of having a hostile relationship with the Drama teacher, Ed Grissom, who, according to Jan, told Jan he had no future as an actor.

Charlie Oncea, one of Jan's surfing buddies, was also in the club, and it was Charlie and Janet who were directly responsible for Jan's first acting role, when they conspired to convince Jan to join them in a production of the play *Stray Cats* (also known as *Stray Cats: A Farce-Comedy in Three Acts*), an unheralded comedy play by Leslie Carter—which was first published in 1925—that they were set to appear in.

The play, which has since fallen into near obsolescence, follows a young photographer, who is poised to inherit millions of dollars from his recently deceased aunt, only on the condition that he is married by midnight of the day he receives the news of his inheritance. He then proceeds to become engaged to three girls, who compare notes about him throughout the story. It's not a very good play.

Charlie and Janet were cast as the Bride and Groom, Tom Skinner and Leona Brooks, in the production, which required someone, a warm body, to play the role of Reverend Patterson, the priest who marries their characters in the story. Enter Jan, or Jan Vincent as he was credited, Jan's name appearing five names down in the credits, underneath Jim Casados but directly above Janet.

Charlie suggested to Janet that Jan would be good for the part, telling Janet to do and say anything to get Jan to take the part. Jan took the role of Reverend Patterson, and on opening night delivered his four lines of dialogue, in a nervous, stammering performance, his uncertain manner drawing laughs from the undemanding, unsophisticated crowd in attendance, which was his only job. It was his first and last comedic role.

5
C's Get Degrees

Although Jan, Jan Vincent, was one of the quietest of the 370 or so members of the Class of 1963, he easily became the most famous over time, which explains why so many of his classmates now claim ownership of so many disparate pieces of his life in Hanford.

This is, of course, a testament to the distorted connection between fame and obscurity, between those who are destined to be in the spotlight, cocooned inside a circle of light, and those who believe they are condemned to stand at the corner of the stage. His tragedy is their revenge, and the reassurance they've taken from his downfall is apparent in their tone and words, even as they express such dismay and grief over where he is today.

The 1963 prom was held in the school cafeteria, which the juniors, as was the tradition, tried to turn into a fantasy land for the graduating seniors, who found it difficult to observe the end of their union in the place where they were all used to eating lunch. Many didn't even attend the Hanford prom, while others, like Jan, left early and went cruising and drinking. When Jan awakened on Monday morning, he was greeted in his bedroom by Lloyd, who issued Jan a stern ultimatum: Work for me at the sign shop, or move out of the house and find your own way in life.

Jan spent part of the summer of 1963 working for Lloyd, earning seventy-five cents an hour painting and installing road signs on the sweltering edges of the county roads, as well as silk-screening posters at the shop. He spent the rest of the summer surfing with Charlie, Frank, and Monty, and dealing with the end of his relationship with Janet, who broke up with him because she was going away to college. Jan was left heartbroken by Janet, who quickly moved on from him, which drove him crazy.

It was the breakup with Janet combined with the collapse of his dream Mexican surfing adventure with the guys in the summer of 1963 that drove Jan away from Hanford after graduation, more than the 100 degree heat he'd endured hauling the signs up and down the roads. Most of Jan's classmates, the ones who continued their educations after high school, enrolled at the nearby College of the Sequoias in Visalia, so when Jan decided to enroll at Ventura College, 200 miles away from Hanford, to move to an area of California in which he had no friends, it was viewed as a bold, gutsy statement of independence.

He chose Ventura College because it was close enough to the ocean so he could surf as often as he wanted to, and because he felt that the distance from Hanford would help him forget about Janet, who attended college in Santa Barbara, only about thirty miles away. They kept in touch, sporadically, through letters and phone calls, for several years, their correspondence extending through the end of the decade and into the early 1970s, when Jan, in one of their last conversations, tried to describe the process in which he was learning how to be a star.

Jan, top row, center, stands to the right of Janet Odell, his high school sweetheart. Their breakup was a major factor in Jan's decision to leave Hanford after high school. (Photo courtesy of Leighton Gould)

Jan, who declared himself to be an art major as a freshman, started classes in August 1963, a career as a commercial artist a vague goal for Jan, much clearer than acting was throughout the rest of 1963 and all of 1964. Jan never gave a second thought to the possibility of an acting career, to the germ that had presented itself to him back in Hanford, until his life as a college student, which ultimately lasted from August 1963 to April 1965, ended and he was left with no other options.

Jan, who bleached his hair blonde as a freshman, painted during his freshman year, but the results were not at all promising. As the freshman year inched forward, Jan, unsurprisingly, began spending more time at the beaches, surfing, and less time in his classes, most of which he performed just adequately in. Jan became increasingly dispirited with his future prospects, fearing the thought of crawling back to Hanford to work for his father, a scenario that nearly played itself out in 1966, after Jan completed the technical training section of the Guard program in Alabama. This likely would've been his fate, even if he had remained at Ventura College for the full four years and earned a degree.

Jan's blonde look only amplified his physical beauty, which was much more appreciated in this environment than it had ever been in Hanford. He lived in an off-campus housing project, made friends very quickly, and dated several girls in his freshman year, none of whom dented his heart, or his imagination, his only romance, during freshman year, taking place with the VW he bought and fawned over. He was, for the first time in his life, being noticed.

The most significant event at Ventura College for Jan took place in the fall of 1964, during Jan's first, and last, semester as a sophomore, when a friend of Jan's suggested that Jan should meet Bonnie Poorman, a dark and silky-haired girl, who was also a student at Ventura College, Bonnie studying art, specializing in pottery and stone sculpting. She had a bewitching aura, though what captivated Jan was her independent spirit, which he bonded with immediately. When Jan first approached her, about the possibility of her attending a beach party he was hosting, she flatly rejected him.

Jan blossomed physically between
Hanford and Ventura College.

One night, Bonnie, whose father was an airline pilot, came over to Jan's dwelling after attending a concert with a date. They started talking, and they were inseparable from then on, the two of them forming a blithe couple, unfamiliar with the Establishment that everyone around them seemed to be into, blissfully ignorant about politics. Bonnie accompanied Jan on his weekend trips back to Hanford, and when Jan first introduced Bonnie to Doris and Lloyd, they quickly voiced their approval.

By January 1965, after Christmas break and prior to the start of the spring semester, Jan's relationship with Bonnie had intensified to the point where marriage was within view. This frightened him; he envisioned the kind of husband he would've made Bonnie then—looking ahead to their passionate but ultimately star-crossed future together.

Jan had also been working at Kane's Men's Wear, a men's store in Oxnard, where he met Lionel Boix, a dashing Australian surfer, who told Jan—who wore a suit and a striped necktie at the store, which sold surfing gear—that he was planning to drive to Mexico to surf and live on the beach, for an unspecified period of time. They became immediate friends, which led to Lionel inviting Jan, stoking the thirst Jan still held from the aborted Mexican trip Jan and his high school friends envisioned in the summer of 1963.

Before Jan decided to run away with Lionel, Jan rolled and wrecked his beloved VW, which happened after Jan had swerved to avoid hitting a brick wall. Days later, as Jan was standing in line to register for the spring semester, he asked himself what he'd been doing at college and what possible good was going to result from staying. There was no reply. He walked away and packed a bag. When Jan and Lionel left for Mexico, they had 200 dollars between them, which was supposed to last for six months.

Jan's parents were horrified by the news, and so was Bonnie, who was given no warning of such a drastic, sudden move by Jan. He left her with the words "I'll keep in touch," and then he walked out on her.

6
The First Wave

When Jan and Lionel arrived in Mexico, in January 1965, they settled in San Blas, a small fishing village on Mexico's West Coast, where they constructed a grass hut on a deserted stretch of beach, which became Jan's home for the next six months.

When they weren't surfing or exploring the dense jungle, Jan and Lionel—who figured they could ration out the 200 dollars they had between them at a rate of a dollar a day during the six month period—survived by catching seafood and helping the local fishermen haul in their nets, in return for scraps. Lionel grew tired of this life very quickly and eventually took off for Hawaii, leaving Jan, who bought a ten-year-old station wagon during his stay in Mexico, to fend for himself.

He wasn't alone for very long. After Lionel's departure, about two months after Jan's arrival in Mexico, a group of hippies found Jan's secluded beach and settled in. They'd brought drugs with them, namely LSD, but Jan was more interested in observing their ways, and he became interested in their ideas about mind expansion. What Jan saw in the hippies made him look at himself more clearly and made him realize that the life he was attempting to pursue away from civilization, and idleness in general, was dishonest and futile.

Jan, who maintained sparse contact with Bonnie and his parents while in Mexico, experienced a rude awakening on several fronts when he returned to California in July 1965. Expecting to find Bonnie, and the status of their relationship, unchanged upon his return, he was shocked to discover that Bonnie had moved on with her life, away from him. She had a new boyfriend, was working in a real estate office, and was planning to leave California for a job caring for the children of people who were about to sail around the world on a yacht.

Jan was also, at this point, carrying the knowledge that he'd been designated 1-A by the United States Army, on account of his dropping out of college, which meant that he was eligible for immediate and unrestricted military service. Several months prior to his military induction, Jan, whose time at Fort Ord officially began on November 29, 1965, found, as a result of his father's contacts, temporary work at an advertising agency in Los Angeles, where he performed basic chores related to his sparse knowledge of commercial art techniques. It was this connection that set Jan on the path to acting and fame, and, some believe, all of his problems.

The head of the ad agency, Robert Black, immediately reckoned that Jan was more suited to starring in commercials than manufacturing them, though Jan, unlike most of his acting contemporaries, never appeared in any commercials during his brief and accelerated Hollywood apprenticeship.

A meeting was arranged for Jan with legendary talent agent Richard "Dick" Clayton, a former actor whose career as a talent agent began in 1951, when Clayton befriended James Dean, when they worked together on the film *Sailor Beware* (1952). Clayton represented Dean until Dean's death in 1955, after which Clayton went on to shepherd the careers of future stars Angie Dickinson, Farrah Fawcett, Jane Fonda, Harrison Ford, Nick Nolte, Burt Reynolds, and many more.

Following Dean's death, Clayton, partly out of tribute to his friend but mostly due to his own Hollywood education, vowed to remake Dean, not in terms of trying to replicate Dean's singular presence and talent but through a purely physical, visual reproduction.

Clayton was a disciple of Henry Willson, the notorious talent agent who specialized in plucking good-looking hunks out of obscurity, then grooming and repackaging them for stardom. Willson, who was gay, pimped out his young male clients, whether they were gay or not, to Hollywood's power brokers, trading sexual favors in exchange for publicity and roles. Willson's most prominent and successful discovery was Rock Hudson, who was a mailman named Roy Scherer when Willson met and seduced him.

If Jan had, like Hudson, started his acting career in the late 1940s instead of 1966, he would've been the ideal Willson client, because of his body and his looks, obviously, and although Jan, unlike Hudson and so many other Willson clients, never had to rely on his penis, which was fat and fleshy, to further his career, there were many other humiliations to follow.

Clayton, who was also gay but maintained a sterling reputation in Hollywood until his death in 2008, didn't engage in such lurid activities, but he did follow Willson's strategy of discovering the young hunks and then grooming them for stardom by presenting them as male models, and as teen idols, regardless of their age.

When Jan signed with Clayton, in the summer of 1966, Clayton's most prized stud was Burt Reynolds, who was then toiling on television and in lackluster movie roles, still several years away from superstardom. Jan was placed alongside future stars Harrison Ford—Ford made his acting debut in the film *Dead Heat on a Merry-Go-Round* (1966)—and Nick Nolte, who started his career as a male model in the late sixties.

Clayton saw so much star potential in Jan that Clayton eventually made Jan his primary focus, to the exclusion of Ford, Nolte, and virtually every other male client on his roster—save for Burt Reynolds. Ford—awkward, stiff Harrison Ford—and Nolte ended up seeking representation elsewhere. Clayton believed that Jan was the next James Dean.

He told Jan as much during that first meeting in Clayton's office, which only made Jan feel more awkward and uncomfortable than he'd been as soon as he arrived, Jan failing to understand what Clayton saw in him, embarrassed, feeling as if he was wasting Clayton's time, while also dreading the start of basic training in late November.

Clayton gained Jan's respect and trust when he revealed that he'd served in the military, during World War II, a fact which also endeared Clayton to Lloyd, who warmed immediately to the idea of Clayton representing Jan, who still didn't take the idea seriously at this point, eventually excusing himself by mentioning his army commitment.

Jan was marketed as a male model and teen idol up until he was in his early thirties.

Jan's evasiveness didn't deter Clayton, who followed Jan on his way out of Clayton's office, pleading with Jan to contact him again, when Jan was free of his army commitment. Jan agreed to do this, but he had little intention of following through. He just wanted to get out of there.

In November, just a few weeks before his induction, Jan was back in Hanford for a visit, when he received a frantic phone call from a teary-sounding Bonnie, begging Jan to come see her in Jackson Hole, Wyoming, where she was working as a waitress, waiting to set sail.

Jan hitchhiked all the way to Jackson Hole, where he was greeted with rejection and surprise by Bonnie, who never believed he would make the trip and wanted nothing to do with him, despite what she'd told him over the phone. The trip was not wasted however; as fate would have it, *The Monroes*, a Western television series, which aired on ABC between 1966 and 1967, was being filmed in Jackson Hole while Jan was there.

After being rebuffed by Bonnie, Jan spent two additional days watching cast members Michael Anderson, Jr. and Barbara Hershey film scenes, the filming process alien to Jan, who hadn't seen actors of any kind work since his minor participation in the ill-fated production of *Stray Cats*, back at Hanford High.

7
The Experiment

Jan's term at the Fort Ord base, which lasted from November 29, 1965 to January 21, 1966, was uneventful, except for the awesome sight of Jan with a shaved head, a transformation he would repeat several years later for the made-for-television film *Tribes* (1970). Fort Ord, which closed in 1994, was cold and gray outside but hot in the barracks, and the base was in the throes of a meningitis outbreak when Jan was there, making daily life miserable for Jan and his comrades in Company D, forcing them to take the bed rolls outside and constantly open the windows, which made the barracks feel wet inside when they went to sleep. While at Fort Ord, Jan received a letter from Bonnie, in which she told him that she'd gotten off the yacht in San Diego. He didn't write back to her.

After basic training, Jan ended up in Alabama, at Fort Rucker, and received his technical training in helicopter maintenance and repair, though he never learned to become a pilot. He later said that his time in the army gave him a stronger sense of self-identity than he'd ever had before and gave him confidence, none of which translated to his acting career and later life. Jan—who remained in the National Guard, in a reserve capacity, until 1971—received an achievement award at the end of his stay at Fort Rucker, but his time in the service hadn't solved any of his inner problems.

After Fort Rucker, Jan headed for Nassau for a period of convalescence, surfing, tormented about his future, assuming that he could still join Lloyd in the family business. When he returned to California, Hanford, and told Lloyd he was willing to enter the sign painting business, Lloyd told Jan he didn't want him there. This rejection, which stunned Jan, led Jan back to Clayton in Los Angeles. When Jan had told Clayton he'd never thought about acting as a career, it was the truth. Now he started.

Clayton was thrilled to see Jan again and immediately decided, as Clayton had done with Harrison Ford, to take Jan to Universal Studios to meet with Monique James, the venerable head of Universal's New Talent Program, one of the first women to hold a position of real authority in Hollywood, the gatekeeper of Hollywood's last contract actors' system. Jan entered Universal's development program in the fall of 1966.

The first role Clayton secured for Jan wasn't at Universal, though it materialized there. As Clayton and Jan were waiting in James' outer office, Clayton was told that Robert Conrad, then star of the CBS television series *The Wild Wild West*, was set to make an independent western feature in Mexico and was looking for a young actor of Jan's age and look to play a supporting role.

After excusing themselves to James, Clayton took Jan to the CBS Studio Center, where Jan met with Conrad, who proceeded to put Jan through the barest of screen tests—look this way, turn left, turn right, say this line, tell me your name. Beyond this, Conrad's only requirement of Jan was that Jan be able to ride a horse, which Jan, who had grown up around horses on his grandparents' farm in Hanford, promised he could, the first line Jan delivered with real conviction.

The film was called *The Bandits* (1967), and Jan was cast in the role of Taye 'Boy' Brown, one of the three cowboy mercenaries—alongside Conrad and grizzled character actor Roy Jenson—who, after escaping a hangman's noose in the film's opening sequence, end up joining their Mexican rescuer on various adventures, which take place against the backdrop of the Mexican revolution.

The start of filming on *The Bandits*, which began shooting in July 1966, was delayed, which left Jan some time to kill before he had to leave for Mexico. Jan, needing a temporary place to stay in Los Angeles, reconnected with a friend from Ventura College, who had an apartment with three rooms, one of which was spare.

When Jan was introduced to his friend's other roommate, Jan was reunited with Bonnie, who was going out with the roommate at the time. Startled by this twist of fate, the reconciliation between Jan and Bonnie progressed rapidly, and they were living together by the time Jan left for Mexico to begin work on *The Bandits*. Jan's sudden move to acting elicited a shocked reaction from Bonnie, who became increasingly supportive once the idea settled.

For his work on *The Bandits*, Jan received 400 dollars per week, plus a modest per diem, for the five weeks of filming. Jan holds up well in the film, delivering his few lines with sincerity, always listening and watching. This impressed Conrad, who set a good example for Jan. Jan took from Conrad an appreciation and enthusiasm for the craft of acting, none of which survived the cynical lessons that Jan received later on from Charles Bronson and Robert Mitchum.

The Bandits was, is, a routine, workmanlike western, indistinguishable from so many others that were released in the late sixties, in and out of Hollywood. Its main purpose, other than introducing Jan, was to facilitate the translation of Conrad's popularity on television to the big screen, which wasn't in the cards. The film went unreleased in North America until 1979.

Besides marking Jan's acting debut, *The Bandits* also changed his name, partially. It was Conrad who, during a break in filming one day, suggested to Jan—who had intended to bill himself, professionally, as Jan Vincent—that Jan, whose character is killed during the film's climatic shootout, should adopt a more masculine name if he wanted to be successful in Hollywood. Hence Jan resurrected his buried middle name, which he thought he'd lost for good in Hanford.

"Listen, kid," Conrad began, putting his arm around Jan on the Mexican location, where more than half of the crew didn't speak English. "You're going to be in this business a long time. You've got to have a man's name."

Then Jan became Michael.

Part Two

Stand and Deliver

1967-1973

"That's the kind of actor he was."

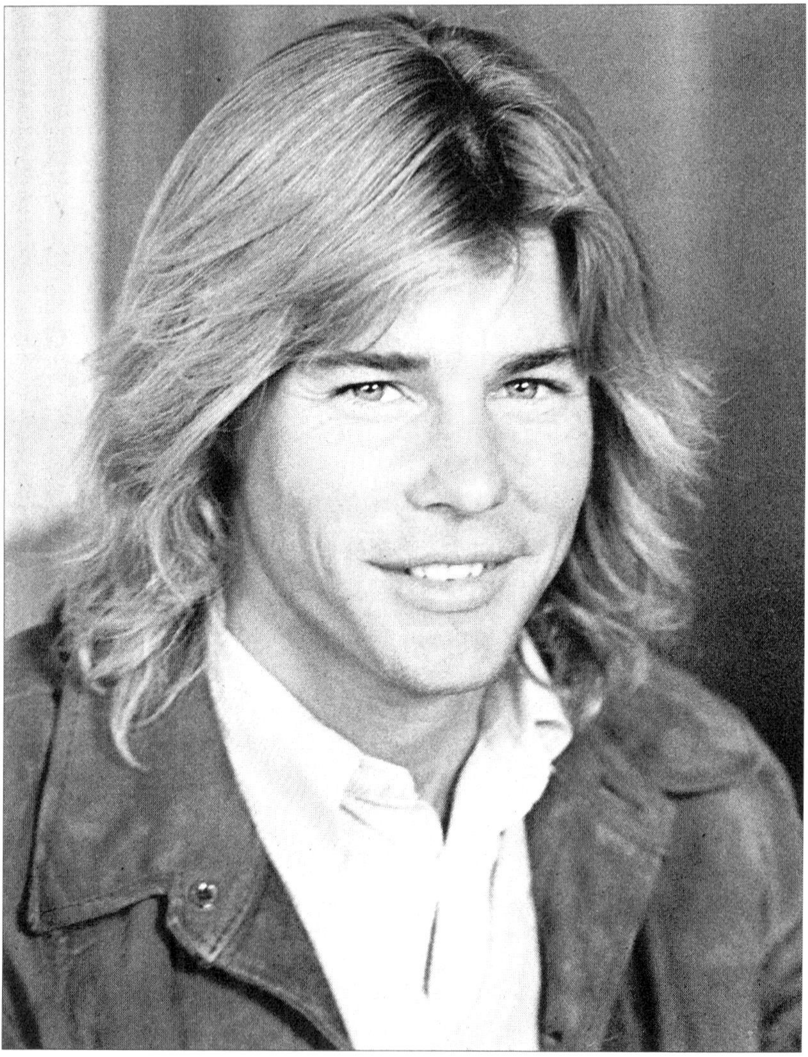

1
Pay or Play

When Jan entered Universal Studios' new talent program in the fall of 1966, the program was billed as the world's largest talent school but operated more like a sausage factory.

Universal's contract system—which officially ended in 1982, when the contract of actress Sharon Gless, who was Hollywood's last contract player, expired—wasn't as controlling, when Jan arrived, as it had been in previous decades. Yet it was still an extremely stifling environment, which was why Jan, who collected $200 per week during the beginners' phase of the program, resisted the idea of a contract, which was acceptable to Monique James, up until the point when Jan started working.

The only discovery Jan made about himself during the acting lessons, which consisted of a battery of screen tests, was that he possessed a photographic memory, or close to it. This was a trait that was invisible to him before he arrived at Universal and one that had never served him in his life, until he was forced to memorize pages of dialogue, which he did with ease.

The only major handicap that was evident during Jan's initial screen tests at Universal was with the physical aspects of acting—he had difficulty understanding marks, how and where to hit them during a scene, and he didn't know where to put his hands and legs, which were constantly restless, like the rest of him.

With the camera always positioned above his shoulders, as he played stock scenes with other contract players, this was easy to overlook. Dick Clayton and Monique James were very pleased, especially Clayton, who saw nothing in Jan that counterbalanced the aura of stardom he'd sensed during their first meeting in 1965.

Jan displayed keen instincts in front of the camera; he had an uncanny feel for what the main point, the heartbeat, of any given scene was and how to bring the underlying message to the surface, often without dialogue—with a look, a pause, silence. He could project emotions—anger, calm, or happiness—on cue, an illusion that dazzled Clayton and James, who were much more impressed by Jan's early results than they had been with Harrison Ford, who was projected to be nothing more than a number three or four supporting player. Jan was a natural.

Jan's training phase officially ended in March 1967, when Jan landed his first role at Universal, in *Journey to Shiloh* (1968), a would-be epic western feature, set during the Civil War, in which Jan was cast as Little Bit Lucket, one of seven young Texans in the film, all part of the Confederate Army, who ride toward the titular location in Tennessee, where a major battle is about to take place.

Jan's promotion to full contract status elevated his salary to $500 per week and made him—like everyone else in his position, including all of his costars in the film—a Pay or Play actor. This meant that he was paid his weekly salary whether he worked or not, an arrangement that instilled a mercenary attitude in the Universal contract players and did not benefit Jan, who was already predisposed to isolation and didn't need any further encouragement to move in this direction.

Journey to Shiloh was based on a well regarded novel by author Will Henry, which is an anti-war novel in the guise of a western. Anti-war sentiment was spreading throughout the film and television industry in the late sixties, and the liberal filmmakers who wanted to express this sentiment in their work—which the western genre, with its devotion to myths and symbolism, was ideal for—were drawn to complicated, rough, unhandsome faces, not the pretty boys like Jan, whose looks—which had served as the whole of his calling card—were viewed, within this corner of Hollywood, as a handicap. Serious filmmakers were only interested in types like Jan—who was Blonde Jan when he shot *Journey to Shiloh*—if they were looking for a psychopath, which may have been the role that Jan was born to play.

Although Universal viewed *Journey to Shiloh* as an epic western, to be shot in Technicolor, the film's modest trappings belied this unrealistic ambition. The film was largely shot on the Universal lot, with additional filming taking place in Agoura and Thousand Oaks, and none of these settings succeeded in evoking the grizzled, weary Southern locations, and the horrors, that inspired the novel.

Jan's early publicity photos

Journey to Shiloh is a more expensive version of *The Bandits, Journey to Shiloh* set against the backdrop of the American Civil War. The other major difference is that the death of Jan's character is presented on film, with a yawning close-up, whereas the death of Jan's character in *The Bandits*, which is barely noticed in the film, happens off screen.

The filming of *Journey to Shiloh*, which was a tortuous process that lasted four months, began in the first week of April, under the direction of William Hale, a tired old warhorse, a television director, whose blunt, plodding sensibilities and vision—which were drilled into him by Universal, with the various edicts they imposed on their television directors—defined the finished product, whose only legacy is its fateful and lengthy pedigree.

Jan's fellow Civil War cowboys—the naïve wanderers, whose journey is accompanied by a rising body count and shrouded by the atrocities they witness along the way, again like *The Bandits*—are played by Michael Burns, James Caan, Harrison Ford, Paul Petersen, Michael Sarrazin, Don Stroud—all Universal contract players, all in the Pay or Play program, which did not bridge the chasm between them and Jan, which widened throughout the filming.

First, there was Jan's inexperience, which wasn't exposed in the film itself, certainly not when Jan filmed his character's death scene—it is a prolonged, thrashing death, a result of fever, which Jan portrays quite effectively. It was, however, very visible to his costars, more in terms of psychology than acting. "Jan was distant and overmatched," recalls Petersen. "We did a script reading, all of us, before the start of filming, and, during the reading, with all of us sitting around the table, James Caan, who was the leader of the pack, told us that, for this to work, we all had to get along and become a team. Jan wasn't part of our group; he fell away from the rest of us and stood apart. As far as his acting, it was obvious that he'd just come out of the beginners' program."

The relationship between Jan and his costars, all of whom were taken by bus to the filming location every morning, showed little improvement throughout the filming, though he did establish a friendship, over time, with Don Stroud, who counted Jan as a friend for many years. "Jan was, essentially, a misfit, and that was his downfall," says Petersen. "He didn't have a very likeable personality, during *Journey to Shiloh*, but the bigger problem with Jan was in how he just kind of tuned out of everything. I also think he had low self-esteem and didn't like himself very much."

Journey to Shiloh wasn't released until May 1968, and the film was greeted with lackluster grosses and reviews. Following his work on *Journey to Shiloh*, Jan, who remained a blonde through 1967 and into 1968, appeared in an episode of the television series *Dragnet 1967*, entitled "The Grenade,"

(September 14, 1967) in which he plays a teenager, a high school student, who has acid thrown on his back in a movie theater.

Then Jan asked Universal for his release.

2
The Independent

After leaving his Universal contract, Jan moved to the 20th Century Fox lot, briefly, to film a one hour pilot, entitled *The Hardy Boys: The Mystery of the Chinese Junk* (September 8, 1967), which was based on the 1959 novel of the same name. The pilot aired on NBC and went unsold.

The *Hardy Boys* pilot represented a second attempt—a serial aired in the 1950s, and three more incarnations followed the 1967 pilot—to transfer the long-running *Hardy Boys* book series, which was plagued by declining sales in 1967, to television. Richard Gates and Tim Matheson starred, respectively, as young adult sleuths Frank and Joe Hardy, while Jan, who was credited as Mike Vincent, was given the role of Tony Prito, a friend of the brothers, the son of Italian immigrants, who is described in the books as a handsome eighteen-year-old with brown eyes, curly black hair, and olive skin. Jan was twenty-three years old.

After the *Hardy Boys* pilot, Jan returned to episodic television for a new incarnation of *Lassie*, which consisted of three thirty minute episodes and was treated as a pilot, though it was, technically, an addendum to the already existing series' fourteenth season—this version offered new characters, a new setting, and a new dog.

Jan had no trouble identifying with his character's environment—his character's name is Chris Hanford, a reference to Jan's hometown and Jan's younger brother, and the show is set in the fictional town of Hanford's Point. The autobiographical references were born out of casual conversations Jan had with the series' producers and writers, in which he described his early life in Hanford—just the facts, no details.

Tony Dow, who played Drew Hanford, Jan's older brother in the episodes, recalls that Jan, who used blue eye drops to accentuate his eyes during filming, was aloof and preferred to be alone, repeating the same tepid response Jan had received, out of his earshot, from his costars during the filming of *Journey to Shiloh*. "Jan was very athletic but struggled with movement," recalls Dow, who is best known as the star of the television series *Leave it to Beaver*. "He wasn't sure where to put his hands and feet. Beyond that, he always seemed unhappy."

Jan's *Lassie* episodes aired on CBS in March 1968, and did not perform well enough, in the eyes of the network, to prompt CBS to continue with this new formula.

Dow, who was also enrolled in the National Guard program, met Jan again in the summer of 1968, when they were both present at Camp San Luis Obispo for reserve duty, which resembled a summer camp environment. "Jan acted like he didn't even know who I was," recalls Dow. "When you work on a show, even a show that gets cancelled, there's a bond that develops and continues over time, but not with Jan. He just blew me off, which kind of shocked me. After we attended summer camp, the next time I saw Jan was at Avila Beach. I saw Jan, who was sitting by himself, on the rocks. I walked right by him, and he didn't say anything to me—this was after we'd done the show together and had been to the National Guard camp."

Jan began 1968 on television, appearing in an episode of the long-running western television series *Bonanza*, entitled "The Arrival of Eddie," (May 19, 1968) with Jan playing the role he was sentenced to throughout this period—the angry, confused but well-meaning young renegade in desperate need of a father figure, or a good woman. Jan was provided with the latter when he reappeared, as a different character, in a 1969 episode of *Bonanza*, entitled "The Unwanted," (April 6, 1969) in which Jan's love interest was played by Bonnie Bedelia, whom he was later paired with in the made-for-television film *Sandcastles* (1972).

In May 1968, Jan, who made his first appearance in the pages of the teen magazine *Tiger Beat* in 1968, returned to Mexico, this time for a legitimate reason, which was not the silly television project he filmed there but rather his impromptu marriage to Bonnie.

Lost at sea: Danger Island. (Photo courtesy of Kim Kahana www.kahanastunts.com)

The television series was *Danger Island*, a live-action adventure serial, which was filmed, over the course of seven weeks, in and around Acapulco, as a three hour block, which was then chopped up into eighteen ten minute segments, which aired on Saturday morning television between September 1968 and January 1969, as part of NBC's one hour children's variety program *The Banana Splits Adventure Hour*.

(Photo courtesy of Kim Kahana www.kahanastunts.com)

Jan was cast as Lincoln "Link" Simmons, an explorer stranded on a tropical island, which is crawling with cannibals, pirates, and all sorts of wild animals. Jan is joined on his quest by an archeologist, who is Jan's superior, and the archeologist's lovely daughter, whom Link is immediately attracted to, this matching the character description of every role Jan played between the late sixties and the early seventies.

Jan's decision to propose to Bonnie, like their decision to hold their wedding on the beach, was entirely spontaneous. Neither the proposal nor the idea of getting married had been at all central in his thoughts when he first arrived in Mexico for *Danger Island*, which was directed by future Hollywood titan Richard Donner.

Jan and Bonnie in Acapulco, Mexico, in July 1968, following their impromptu wedding.

The news of Jan's impending marriage quickly spread to the cast and crew—with whom Jan was much closer than he had been on *The Bandits* and *Journey to Shiloh*—at the end of the filming schedule, in July, when the girlfriends and wives of the almost entirely male cast and crew were flown into

Acapulco to join their partners. "The casting director told me that Bonnie and Jan were going to get married right there," recalls costar and stuntman Kim Kahana, who played Chongo in the serial and later reunited with Jan on the film *The Mechanic* (1972). "There was no planning; it was entirely spontaneous on Jan's part. The cast and crew gathered around this grass shack, near the beach, which was where the ceremony took place. I was Jan's best man."

**Jan with friend and *Danger Island* costar Kim Kahana.
(Photo courtesy of Kim Kahana www.kahanastunts.com)**

Beyond July 1968, when filming ended on *Danger Island*, there is no precise date of marriage to compare here—there was no wedding certificate and no record of the ceremony, or the vows, which were handwritten by Bonnie and Jan, just prior to the ceremony, which was presided over by a tribal mayor, an old Indian witch doctor, who blessed the marriage by daubing paint on Bonnie and Jan's faces.

Any suggestion of the marriage being invalid, an issue which was briefly raised during Bonnie and Jan's otherwise amicable separation in 1976, withered by the time they returned to California, where they registered as man and wife.

Part Two: Stand and Deliver 1967-1973

Jan and Kim Kahana with their *Danger Island* costar Ronne Troup.
(Photos courtesy of Kim Kahana www.kahanastunts.com)

Jan (right) behaves fearlessly during a break in filming.
(Photo courtesy of Kim Kahana www.kahanastunts.com)

They never took further steps toward a formal marriage ceremony, which meant there was no need for a divorce when they broke apart, only a new definition for their living arrangement, which continually evolved throughout the marriage.

There was a commitment.

3
American Idol

In February 1969, Jan returned to Mexico, this time visiting Durango to begin work on the film *The Undefeated* (1969), a 20th Century Fox production, another western. *The Undefeated* starred Rock Hudson and John Wayne, the first two Hollywood icons Jan encountered in his never-ending apprenticeship.

Jan's career in the following decade was almost entirely defined by this dynamic, and most of the icons he appeared alongside—Darren McGavin and Burt Reynolds were notable exceptions—turned out to be very bad role models for Jan, who needed mentoring as much as he needed to at least familiarize himself with the fundamentals of acting technique.

Hudson and Wayne were both in weakened states by the time Jan reached them. For Hudson—this was about fifteen years before the ravages of AIDS took hold of the public's perception of him—this was related to his film career, which had lost momentum and was nearing its end, heralding a move to television in the early 1970s. Hudson established a successful second career on television in the 1970s, which brought him a measure of security but not renewal. Jan, who found himself in the same position in the early eighties, found this part of Hudson's story very instructive.

Wayne, who remained a box office draw into the early seventies, was at the beginning of a decade-long farewell tour; he received his lifetime achievement award in the form of the best actor Oscar he was gifted for *True Grit* (1969), the film Wayne shot prior to *The Undefeated*.

Jan dreaded working with Wayne, which owed less to a justified sense of awe and more to Wayne's perceived far right wing political leanings, views that Jan believed, if put into action, would create a fascist America. Jan, who voiced his opposition to the Vietnam War in 1969 in several print interviews, didn't hold Wayne—"the biggest of the stars," as Jan later called him—responsible for the war but recognized the importance of this symbol and intended to make Wayne the focal point of Jan's misplaced anger. When Jan met Wayne, and he discovered that the man more than lived up to the legend, Jan almost wet his pants.

Jan's limited political beliefs were entirely shaped by those around him. By the dawn of 1969, Jan's sister, Jacquie, was a veteran of the Haight-Ashbury scene, and then there was Lloyd, who, perhaps somewhat surprisingly, had taken a passionate stance against the Vietnam War. In the fall of 1969, Lloyd—who was worried about Christopher, who was in his last year at Hanford High—enlisted Jan's help in finding a good draft lawyer to spare Christopher from conflict—either Guard duty or the war, neither of which Christopher was exposed to.

Jan's preconceptions about Wayne turned out to be unfounded. Although Wayne was an ardent conservative, Jan found him to be friendly, inclusive, and warm, while Jan also made a favorable impression on Wayne, who was very conscious of his mortality at this time, both literally and in terms of his standing as a box office favorite, and was increasingly on the lookout for attractive young actors to complement him and assume some of the heavy lifting he was no longer capable of.

More and more, Wayne, who was dimly nervous at this time about the advance of the faster, younger triggermen—Clint Eastwood, Steve McQueen, followed by Burt Reynolds —poised to overthrow him, seemed open to the possibility of a collaboration with the next generation of actors and filmmakers. However, the role of torch passer was one that Wayne, who was sixty-one when *The Undefeated* started filming, was unable to embrace.

Wayne could not bring himself to appear in a film without occupying its every morsel. He refused to entertain any project, any pairing, that would be regarded as anything other than a John Wayne film, which is not how any collaboration with Eastwood or McQueen would've been viewed at this point in time.

Eastwood and McQueen, who were both born in 1930, are the only superstars from this period—between the late 1960s and the mid-1970s—whom Jan didn't appear with in his career. If Jan, who was born in 1944 but clearly belonged in another dimension of time, had caught Wayne's eye six, seven years later in Jan's career, Jan could've filled the role of the pursuing daredevil—the role he played against Bronson, Reynolds, and so many others—opposite Wayne's aging gunslinger, while not posing the threat to Wayne's status that Eastwood and McQueen surely represented. However, by that time, 1975 or 1976, Jan was on the edge of a precipice, and Wayne was dying.

There's nothing progressive about *The Undefeated*—which was directed by Andrew V. McLaglen, one of several films McLaglen and Wayne made together—or Jan's role in the film. Jan's character, Bubba Wilkes, is a confederate soldier under the command of Hudson's General James Langdon, who, days after the end of the Civil War, leads his confederate army to Mexico, where they cross paths—form an uneasy alliance—with Wayne's Union company. By this time, Bubba has already proposed to Hudson's daughter, Charlotte (Melissa S. Newman), who spends the entire film contemplating the proposal.

Wayne did put Jan's face and name in his mental file, which Wayne retrieved in September 1969, with the intention of employing Jan in Wayne's next western film, *Chisum* (1970), which was also directed by McLaglen. Wayne envisioned Jan for the role of Billy the Kid, a role that Jan—who was committed to start work on *The Survivors*, a television series for Universal—was forced to decline. The fifth place role was instead given to Geoffrey Deuel, who made little of it and was little heard from.

Jan was busy filming *The Survivors* when *The Undefeated* was released into theaters in November 1969, to a middling response, and Jan's disappointment at not getting to work with Wayne a second time may have carried over into his thoughts of the show, which, in itself, was left open to any number of criticisms, and bad chuckles, all well deserved.

The Survivors brought Jan back to Universal, back under contract, the conditions and terms much more favorable than before—he could leave at any time, on a whim.

It was the show Jan hated, so much so that he vowed never to do another television series again, a pledge that lasted close to fifteen years and was only broken when he had nowhere else to turn.

The Survivors is a garish, hysterically overblown nighttime soap opera, inspired by trash merchant author Harold Robbins' bestselling novel of the same name. Jan was cast to appear alongside Lana Turner—another legend, one of the last Women of Hollywood, which is a nice way of saying that everyone thought she was dead long before her obituary was printed in *Variety*. She required a leaning board during the filming of the episodes, which allowed her to rest without sitting while she waited on set.

Turner plays the series' matriarch, Tracy Carlyle Hastings, and Jan, who appeared in eight of the series' total of fifteen episodes, plays her son, Jeffrey Hastings, with whom Tracy maintains a rather unwholesome preoccupation. This is the story of a millionaire, and Jeffrey is revealed to be illegitimate, a bastard, who was conceived years earlier, when his jet-setting mother had an affair with a Greek tour guide.

Jan, who was credited as Michael Vincent, knew very little of this, or anything else that happened, character and story wise, on the show. His scenes with Turner, who was struggling with alcohol, were filmed separately, at Universal, away from the rest of the show. The rest of the scenes were filmed in the south of France, a location Jan never visited throughout his career. *The Survivors*, whose first season budget was a whopping $8 million, aired on ABC between September 1969 and January 1970.

The Survivors left Jan very disillusioned with television, which didn't mean he was free of it, though he left Universal again. The next contract he entered into with the studio, in 1983, was worth millions.

He did not, for the first time in ages, seem so disillusioned with the rest of his life, not since he and Bonnie had married—"we married ourselves" was how Jan described what had transpired between them back in Acapulco.

Bonnie was as far removed from the workings of Hollywood as anyone Jan knew, outside of Hanford and his surfing community, Bonnie preferring to keep busy with her art, especially her pottery. Jan indulged this, sensing how important it was for her to keep busy, as the demands on his time, and his body, increased—the latter almost exponentially, as it turned out.

He would, on occasion, ask her for an opinion on certain scripts, which was the type of conversation he rarely had throughout his relationship with Dick Clayton, who was an expert at discovering and grooming talent but was not so adept at navigating the crucial middle section of a client's career, which was the point when his grateful but restless discoveries left him.

Bonnie and Jan lived in a frame-sided, two bedroom cottage, within an extremely rural, wooded area of Topanga Canyon, way out in the north end of Malibu, secluded from the rest of Malibu by several dirt-rotted roads. Jan later bought a hundred acres of land in Santa Monica, ranch property, on which he intended to build, by hand, a permanent, two-story residence for himself and Bonnie and however many children they had—out of a discarded redwood water tank. The marriage barely survived long enough to see this become a reality.

The Topanga residence, which was somewhat malnourished when Bonnie and Jan moved there, contained orange trees, and Jan, who practiced yoga for a time, later added crops for the purpose of growing organic food. Bonnie and Jan also had a German Shepherd, several horses, a parrot. "Jan's houses were magnificently appointed," recalls Robert Englund, Jan's friend and costar in the film *Buster and Billie*. "That was because Bonnie and Jan had such good taste, artistically, especially Bonnie. There was artwork and turn-of-the-century craftsmanship throughout their homes and lots of Hawaiiana. The craftsman furniture, especially, in Jan's houses was really ahead of its time. You wouldn't have seen that in Barbra Streisand's house, for example, back in the early seventies. Bonnie and Jan—who looked like James Dean when he wore his reading glasses at home—seemed very happy together. Jan was a frustrated musician and loved playing the guitar at home, and Bonnie and Jan threw some wonderful parties, especially at Christmas."

Jan and Bonnie in Malibu.

The number of Jan's appearances in the teen magazines—which is the most telling measure of the level of Jan's celebrity when Jan was in his twenties—spiked in 1969. He appeared twice in *Tiger Beat* and three times in *Fave*, with Jan, who turned twenty-five in July 1969, photographed barechested, looking innocent, describing the boy he used to be and the perfect girl he was looking for.

At this point in his career, Jan appeared alongside Davy Jones and Bobby Sherman, who were both in Jan's age bracket and were nearing the end of their teen idol careers, replaced, in the early seventies, by David Cassidy, Donny Osmond, Richard Thomas, and Jan. Jan remained, as if he was frozen in time, in the teen magazines until August 1976, when he was featured in *16*. He was thirty-two years old.

Jan and Bonnie at home.

4
Local Hero

The made-for-television film *Tribes*, which aired on ABC—as a Movie of the Week—in November 1970, represented the first project and role Jan was proud of, enough to compel him to finally discard the stiff, workmanlike moniker of Michael Vincent in favor of Jan-Michael Vincent. He had reason to be proud; *Tribes* contains his best early performance. Perhaps even more significantly, *Tribes* implanted a belief throughout Hollywood that Jan was a rising star, which lasted about six years.

Tribes was also the first project to make the gang back in Hanford sit up and take notice of Jan as an actor. Several of Jan's former classmates knew he was in Hollywood, and some of the nosy ones were even aware of *The Bandits*. Now, it was becoming obvious that Jan was on the verge of serious recognition, which was a shock for many of them, recalling awkward, shy Jan Vincent from just seven years earlier. "It [*Tribes*] was the first movie that made some of the people in Hanford take notice," recalls Charlie Oncea. "Our reaction was like, 'Oh, he's actually got some talent as an actor.' He gave a really excellent performance in that film, and I think we were all shocked at first that he was capable of that."

Jan's best performances throughout his career came in roles that contained autobiographical details he could easily access and relate to, which was the case, to varying degrees, with the characters he played in *Going Home* (1971), *Buster and Billie* (1974), *White Line Fever* (1975), and *Baby Blue Marine* (1976). The characters in these films all contain elements and traits that can be tied to Jan's basic personality and his life.

No character Jan played throughout his career was as organically-tied to his soul, and whatever belief system lurked there, as Adrian, a young Vietnam era draftee, an anti-war hippie and pacifist, who, as the film opens, grudgingly reports to an army depot for the start of boot camp.

A man of honor: *Tribes* (1970).

The similarities between Jan, who was still in the Guard program when *Tribes* started filming in the summer of 1970, and Adrian are apparent in the opening shot of the film, which is a tight shot on Jan's face, his hair blonde, his lips full and lustrous, staring out the window as he rides along on a bus with his fellow recruits, his face intercut with the visions he has of a girl he is clearly still in love with. Was Jan thinking about Janet, his high school sweetheart?

Jan's time at Fort Ord and Fort Rucker wasn't nearly as grueling as what Adrian and his fellow recruits go through in the film, under the command of two drill instructors, played by Earl Holliman and Darren McGavin, both of whom received higher billing than Jan, who understood the geography of a military post and barely flinched when he and his costars arrived at the barracks in San Diego, where most of the filming took place.

Jan quickly bonded with his costars, a process that was made easy on the second day of filming, when they all had their heads shaved, a transformative moment for all of them, especially Jan, who wasn't a pacifist but despised the Vietnam War. This was a view shared by the entire cast and crew, who noticed that Jan's shaved look brought about a dramatic change in his personality, on and off camera. "Jan became a leader, like the character he played in the film," recalls Danny Goldman, who plays Sidney, the weakling recruit Adrian stands up for in the film. "Jan appeared as a natural born leader on the set, who clearly understood the marine mentality and that way of life. When Jan had his head shaved, it brought out his natural instincts as an actor, in terms of his ability to grasp the central concept and idea within a scene and project it in front of the camera without dialogue. He had a lack of confidence toward the acting process because of his lack of acting experience, so he didn't have the authority and credibility to speak up and let his feelings be known. He didn't understand filmmaking verbiage enough at this point to get his point across, which is why I think he was aloof at times on the set. He would sometimes go off by himself before the filming of scenes."

At first Adrian appears to McGavin's character, Sgt. Drake, as a model recruit: Adrian demonstrates strong leadership and excels at all of the training exercises, except for the rifle practice drills, during which Adrian hesitates and finally withdraws; this serves as the film's main conflict. "Jan was the shy rebel," says Goldman, who later worked with Jan on the film *The World's Greatest Athlete* (1973). "He also had a heroic nature and believed in standing up for the little guy, which was who I played in the film. I was the loser who couldn't do anything right in the film, and Jan was the type who would've stood up for someone like that. Jan was a good athlete and had an easy time with the physical training our characters went through in the film. He definitely shared the beliefs his character held; he was opposed to the war in Vietnam, like the rest of us were. *Tribes* captured the feelings of that time."

The best scene in *Tribes*—and in Jan's career up to this point—happens near the end of the film, after Adrian has deserted the base and run into the nearby town, to a bus depot, where he's found by McGavin, who has grown to respect Adrian's point-of-view, though he doesn't agree with it. In the scene, Jan explains the reasons why he is unable to kill, under any circumstances, while McGavin counters with the argument that killing, war, is necessary in order to preserve the right for two men with such opposing views to be able to have this conversation.

McGavin talks Adrian into returning to the base, but this positive military influence is offset by the real villain of the piece, Holliman's obstinate

Sgt. DePayster. DePayster denies Adrian the opportunity to graduate because of Adrian's failure to perform at the rifle practice, and he designates Adrian for "special" retraining. The knowledge of this compels Adrian to go AWOL, leaving behind Drake, who pays tribute to Adrian by pinning up a sketch of a seagull as a reminder of Adrian, before he dutifully goes to face another batch of recruits.

Jan later said that *Tribes*, which was directed by Joseph Sargent, captured all of his feelings toward the military, and that he would have done the film for nothing, sensing, correctly, that the credibility he gained from the film was worth infinitely more than the $25,000 salary he earned for the film.

Tribes, which was nominated for three primetime Emmy awards, was released theatrically in Europe following its American broadcast, which drew excellent ratings for ABC and has now, like so many television films from the 1970s, receded into legend.

When Jan, following the making of *Tribes*, attended his next National Guard session, the commanding officer took one look at Jan's shaved head and accused him of being a smartass.

5
The Man of the Moment

Although Jan's well-received performance in *Tribes* was a turning point in Jan's career, and suggested the possibility of stardom, it did not free him from television, to which he was shackled, sporadically, until the fall of 1974, when Hollywood began a concerted effort to turn Jan into a major Hollywood star, an investment that Jan, and his work, merited briefly. Jan's period as an above-the-line film actor limped along until the fall of 1978, the point when this status, and the well of the resources Hollywood poured into the Jan-Michael Vincent Project, evaporated.

In the fall of 1970, Jan filmed a bit part, an extended cameo, in an episode of the television series *Dan August*, a police detective show starring Burt Reynolds. Reynolds was, at this time, without his soon-to-be trademark moustache, a look he kept for his breakthrough role in the film *Deliverance* (1972), which brought Reynolds, after more than a decade on television, film stardom, which was at its peak when Jan and Reynolds later reunited for the film *Hooper* (1978), a box office hit for Reynolds, a validation of his bankability, which did nothing for Jan's career.

A discombobulated and shaggy-looking Jan plays a peripheral murder suspect in the episode, entitled "Death Chain," Jan's character functioning as a red herring, which is how Jan increasingly felt, in terms of how he was portrayed, throughout the seventies.

After *Tribes*, this did not represent advancement—far from it—but this is what it was like to be a young actor in the early 1970s.

The biggest event for Jan in 1971 was the discovery that Bonnie was pregnant for the first time. She had a miscarriage in April.

In the summer of 1971, Jan appeared on another long-running television western series: *Gunsmoke*. The king of television westerns, *Gunsmoke* was a rite of passage for falling and rising actors alike, Jan following in the footsteps of Bronson, Reynolds, and Jon Voight. Jan's appearance in the episode entitled "The Legend" (October 18, 1971) predated the appearances of Harrison Ford, Jan's former stable-mate, and Richard Dreyfuss, who competed against Jan for the chance to star opposite Bronson in the film *The Mechanic*.

The role of Kevin Colter was perfectly-tailored for Jan, in terms of the roles that the television industry believed Jan, who had been in Hollywood approximately five years, was best-suited for. Kevin is a troubled but well-meaning young man, who brings trouble everywhere he stands, until he stumbles into the redemptive universe of Dodge City, whose forgiving, warm elders—Doc Adams, Kitty, Matt Dillon—make it their mission to preside over Kevin's salvation. This was not unlike the attempts that some of Jan's elders in Hollywood—such as Ernest Borgnine—made when Jan was in his early forties, centered around Jan's use of cocaine (which was not a problem in Dodge City), or with Jan throughout the end of his twenties.

Jan's next feature film role, which he received in the summer of 1971, was the drama *Going Home*, in which Jan was given third billing, behind Brenda Vaccaro, and Robert Mitchum, the next legend to enter Jan's career and life, who showed Jan that it was possible to deliver good work while boozing and womanizing during off hours.

Jan loved Mitchum, who was fifty-four at this point but acted and looked much older when *Going Home* began filming in July 1971, a point in time when Mitchum was looked at as a considerable talent whose magnificent force of presence had, for the most part, been wasted in too many inferior films.

Both *Out of the Past* (1947) and *Night of the Hunter* (1955)—the films that were, and continue to be, looked at as being the definitive, most robust examples of Mitchum's mood and persona, when he was still in his physical prime—had yet to receive their due, which would not be forthcoming until after Mitchum's death in July 1997, when so many of these knucklehead critics and historians finally acknowledged that, yes, he was one of the greatest screen actors of all time.

Going Home arrived in the middle of a resurgence for Mitchum, not commercially but in terms of his legacy, which was enlivened considerably by his strong work in the films *Farewell, My Lovely* (1975), *The Friends of Eddie Coyle* (1973), and *Ryan's Daughter* (1971). These were three of the films that bracketed *Going Home*, a Metro-Goldwyn-Mayer production that unfolded very much like an independent project, which was most evident upon the film's scant theatrical release.

Going Home was filmed on location in McKeesport, Pennsylvania, a depressed Pittsburgh suburb, and in the squalid seaside town of Wildwood, New Jersey. McKeesport, where most of the production was based throughout the two month filming schedule, was populated by all kinds of human oddities, one of whom, a middle-aged woman, broke into Mitchum's motel room while the star was away, and then jumped into his bed and fell asleep, until she was removed. Jan was not yet worthy of such madness, but it was a good lesson for him.

There was also a heat wave, and there were several pollution alerts in McKeesport, throughout the six weeks of filming that took place there, which, along with the presence of Hollywood, further riled the locals, who treated the cast and crew not as humans but humanoids.

Jan's most memorable encounter with Mitchum occurred while they were filming a scene inside a pickup truck, with Jan in the passenger seat and a camera resting on a tray between them. While they were waiting to start shooting the scene, Mitchum shared his career philosophy with Jan, who hung on every word Mitchum said. "Never choose a movie because of the script," Mitchum started, turning toward Jan. "It's the location, kid."

"Yes?" Jan replied.

"I thought I was doing a movie in San Francisco," Mitchum continued. "My agent said yes to the wrong script—this one—and that's how I ended up here. When I found out I was going to be in McKeesport, I fired him."

Then Mitchum lit up a joint for himself, and then one for Jan, who was a pothead at this time and remained so, to varying degrees of intensity, throughout his Hollywood career. Jan's introduction to cocaine took place in the spring of 1975, in Arizona, during the filming of *White Line Fever*, when he was given a sample, and indoctrinated, by a stuntman.

Jan plays Mitchum's son in *Going Home*, which is about a troubled father-son relationship, which was irrevocably damaged after the son witnessed the murder of his mother at the hands of his father at the age of six. While Mitchum's character, Harry Graham, spent thirteen years behind bars, his son, Jimmy, bounced around between foster homes and the walls of bureaucratic ineptitude, growing into an angry young man, seething with ideas about revenge toward his father, who is paroled as the film opens.

The lifelong apprentice: *Going Home* (1971).

The film opens with the murder of the mother, which is seen through the eyes of six-year-old Jimmy—the dying mother appears in front of the camera, following the sounds of a vicious beating, her throat cut, and then she stumbles down the stairs, blood spurting out—instead of placing the camera squarely on young Jimmy's eyes and face, so as to let the event unfold entirely through implication and sound. It's a decidedly tactless, unsavory opening, which alerts the viewer to the real possibility that the film's director, Herbert B. Leonard, will mishandle future scenes. The film is a mess.

Jan, who was twenty-seven when the film was shot, plays a nineteen-year-old in the film, the age difference minor compared to the emotional demands contained within the character, which required Jan to be simultaneously likable and psychotic, a range of emotions the film does not adequately provide a sound psychological foundation for. The tone of the film alternates between reconciliation and tangled rage, with Jimmy appearing more erratic than sympathetic.

This inconsistency of narrative and tone is most apparent in the film's rape scene, where the sexually awkward and inexperienced Jimmy assaults Mitchum's girlfriend, played wonderfully by Vaccaro. The rape sequence is inserted into the film in a thudding manner, without bookending scenes to provide context, and is presented not as the outgrowth of Jimmy's twisted psyche but as the resolution of a domestic argument over where Jimmy should be living.

Jan, as he does in *Tribes*, provides a quiet, simmering presence that could have, in more capable hands, been molded to accommodate all of the elements that existed in Lawrence B. Marcus' fascinating, potent original script, which assembled all of the ingredients for affecting, searing, superior drama, and provided the instructions for this, which were not followed.

Going Home did expose Jan's limitations as an actor, which barely lessened over time, namely his inability to improvise and to, quite simply, create chicken salad out of chicken shit, which is what Mitchum does so effortlessly throughout the film. Or maybe the rest of the film, and the heart of Jan's performance, was left on the cutting room floor.

Jan was angry when he saw the released version of *Going Home* and blamed MGM's abrasive president, James Aubrey, who was known to order severe editorial cuts on MGM films, for reediting a film Jan believed was good and powerful. Jan's hostility over the situation was shared by Leonard, who openly accused Aubrey—who personally trimmed more than twenty minutes from Leonard's filmed version, in order to secure a PG rating—of raping the picture. Mitchum sued MGM over the mishandling of the film, which was released, initially, in Los Angeles in November 1971, with no meaningful promotional campaign or previews. The film quickly disappeared.

There was a silver lining to the making of *Going Home* for Jan, besides the experience of working with Mitchum. This was the Golden Globe nomination Jan received for his performance in the film, in the best supporting actor category, which was emblematic of the Golden Globe committee's dubious selection process throughout the 1970s and 1980s, which did lasting damage to the organization's credibility and influence.

However, Jan was no Pia Zadora.

Jan was beaten out by Ben Johnson from *The Last Picture Show* (1971), a performance that brought Johnson an Oscar win. This was the first recognition of any kind that Jan had received up to this point, both as an actor and in terms of his overall life, not including the achievement ribbon he was given at Fort Rucker.

6
Then Came Bronson

The crime-thriller film *The Mechanic*, which began filming in Los Angeles in November 1971, provided Jan with his first leading role in a feature film, though Jan was dwarfed—in name and stature—by the film's main attraction, Charles Bronson, who was the most private, reserved star Jan encountered during Jan's rocket ship ride throughout the 1970s. Their mutual quietness could have provided the basis for some level of camaraderie and understanding. There was none of this.

Bronson turned fifty on November 3, 1971, right around the start of filming, a most unlikely point for an actor to suddenly become a star, though there was nothing sudden about Bronson, who had been making films since 1951 and was best known, at this point, to North American audiences for his supporting roles in the films *The Dirty Dozen* (1967), *The Great Escape* (1963), and *The Magnificent Seven* (1960). In these films, Bronson's silent, strong presence facilitated Yul Brynner, Lee Marvin, Steve McQueen, and others—it was Bronson's job to perform all of the grimy, thankless tasks these stars considered beneath them.

It was a glaring oversight, lasting twenty years, which was summarily corrected when United Artists, with whom Bronson, who received a salary of $400,000 plus a cut of the profits for *The Mechanic*, entered into a long-term contract in 1971. By 1974, Bronson was commanding $1 million per picture, which was a lot of money then, even for established stars. Jan was paid $50,000 for *The Mechanic*, and only once in his career— *Damnation Alley* (1977)—did his salary eclipse six figures for a single film.

Bronson's hallmark as an actor, both as a supporting player and a leading man, was an insistence on a bare minimum of dialogue, which was well-suited to the unbending mask of competence he projected. It was an approach that served him well as a leading man in the 1970s but made it impossible for Hollywood to place stars of equal or greater stature alongside him.

This was one of the main reasons why Bronson's star period didn't extend far beyond 1977, when his contract with United Artists ended, along with his standing as an American box office draw, though Bronson remained a bankable star overseas for a considerably longer period of time. This was especially the case in the Third World, where most of his later films—the dumb revenge thrillers he willed his career to in the 1980s, for the Cannon Films assembly line—required little or no dubbing.

"You don't get to know him," was how Jan later described the experience of working with Bronson on *The Mechanic*. It was as if Bronson had singled out Jan personally for Bronson's well-known mode of isolation and rigidness, which every costar—especially the few women he allowed to share the screen with him—Bronson allowed to enter his well-guarded domain took away from their encounters with him.

This is why Bronson chose to work so often with the same people, another reason why he was doomed to commercial extinction. *The Mechanic* was one of six films that director Michael Winner made with Bronson, a number surpassed only by J. Lee Thompson, who made nine films with Bronson, including most of the dreary Cannon titles that destroyed Bronson's box office credibility.

This was, like Bronson's character in *The Mechanic*, a man who did not resist change and new ideas so much as he made them disappear. It was this inability to see two, three moves ahead that doomed both of them—Arthur Bishop, the veteran assassin who mentors the protégé who kills him, and Bronson himself, for whom *The Mechanic* marked the beginning of a productive five-year period, in which Bronson starred in a string of films that were enjoyed by critics and moviegoers alike.

The Mechanic provides the clearest template of the apprentice-master dynamic that defined Jan's film career throughout the 1970s. Jan was twenty-seven when he was cast as Steve McKenna, the aspiring contract killer Bronson tutors in the film, who is a hedonist in his early twenties—he only cares about fast cars and girls.

There was supposed to be much more to this relationship. *The Mechanic*'s writer, Lewis John Carlino, originally intended *The Mechanic* to be a dark, gay love story between these two killers—the older assassin and the young apprentice—that explored the theme of sexual manipulation through the chess game that unfolds.

The Mechanic began as a would-be novel, which Carlino abandoned in favor of writing a screenplay, which was completed in the fall of 1967. Carlino sold his script—which attracted the attention of Kirk Douglas and Burt Lancaster in 1967, when Carlino was still polishing the script—to producer Martin Poll in the middle 1968, and in 1969, Cliff Robertson was set to star as Bishop, with Jeff Bridges slotted to play Steve McKenna. Martin Ritt was hired to direct this incarnation, which was to begin shooting in New York in June 1969.

When this fell through, Robertson abandoned the project and was replaced, briefly, by George C. Scott, who, like Robertson, objected to the script's explicit homoerotic content. After Bronson, a staunch conservative, and Winner—who had recently worked together on the western feature *Chato's Land* (1972)—signed on in the summer of 1971, the homosexual parts were phased out of the script. Jan, who had a sizable gay following throughout the 1970s, never saw Carlino's original script and was completely unaware of these changes when filming began.

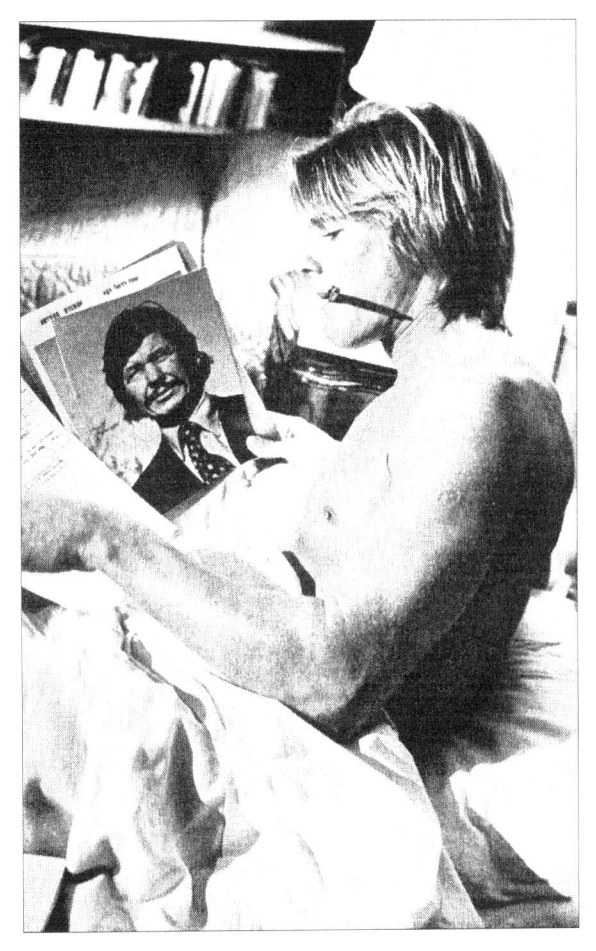

Charles Bronson was Jan's nemesis on screen and off in *The Mechanic* (1972).

It was Winner who later stated, in his 2004 autobiography, that Bronson "hated Jan," an assertion scarcely endorsed by the film's few living cast and crew members, most of whom recall Jan as bringing a cocky attitude to the production. This was very unlike Jan, who was otherwise known to be very deferential and lacking in confidence throughout the 1970s.

The relationship between Bronson and Jan was strained before they met, related to the casting of the Steve McKenna role and Bronson's latent disappointment over not getting the costar he wanted—this was Robert F. Lyons, a general purpose actor, five years younger than Jan, whom Bronson befriended and later cast in several films.

Bronson insisted that Winner grant Lyons an audition, which did not go well. When Bronson inquired about the reasons for Lyons not being hired, Winner deflected the question by suggesting his first choice for Steve, a pre-*American Graffiti* Richard Dreyfuss. Bronson rejected this.

Jan was the compromise. When Winner brought up Jan's name to Bronson, who had never heard of Jan, Winner suggested that Bronson, a decorated World War II veteran, screen *Tribes*, which Bronson found stimulating, in spite of its politics. Conscious of the number of objections he'd already exercised with the film's producers, the team of Robert Chartoff and Irwin Winkler, and the amount of capital he'd expended to get his wife, actress Jill Ireland, cast in the role of a call girl, Bronson relented.

It seems that Jan, like Steve, attempted to take over some of Bronson's responsibilities during filming. Bronson did not need or want any help, unlike Bishop, who is aging, obviously, and in need of a backup. In the film, Bishop and Steve's relationship begins at the funeral of Steve's father, whom Bishop was contracted to kill—he induced a heart attack in the old man. Later, Steve invites Bishop to join him at the home of Steve's troubled girlfriend, who tries to gain Steve's attention by slicing her wrists. When Steve refuses to give in, Bishop begins to realize that Steve is, like himself, someone who lives by a different rule book, which is the code that Jan was in the process of adopting at this time.

The film's explosive, fiery climax was shot during the first week of filming in Los Angeles. Steve has just returned to Los Angeles, alone, from Italy, where he killed Bishop through poisoning. After roaming Bishop's house, possibly with the intention of assuming not only Bishop's career but also his life, Steve goes outside and approaches his red Ford Mustang. When he opens the door to get inside, he sets off a trip wire, which is spelled out to Steve in a letter, written by Bishop, which Steve finds attached to the rear-view mirror. The car explodes. End of film.

This did not sit well with Jan, who made similar miscalculations about Bronson. Jan suggested to Winner—and to the film's stunt coordinator, Kim Kahana, Jan's costar from *Danger Island* and his best man—an alternate version that left open the possibility, however ludicrous, for Steve's resurrection. "I designed the stunt, and Jan told me that he wanted Steve to leave the car, covered in flames, suggesting that he could be alive at the end of the film," recalls Kahana, Bronson's longtime stunt double. "Jan acted very cocky, and it seemed like he was trying to take control of the film, take away some of Bronson's responsibilities, which he lacked the experience to do. I had to put Jan down; I had to take him aside a few times and set him straight."

Bronson, who was intensely germ-phobic, was raised in the harsh coal-mining town of Ehrenfeld, Pennsylvania, a setting that made Bronson fearful of closed spaces and wary of personal contact. The only time Bronson—who was so shy that he had his double, Kim Kahana, sign autographs in Bronson's name when the production was in Los Angeles—took an interest in Jan was when Jan developed a hacking cough during the filming and began sneezing.

"You need to watch that cold, Jan," Bronson said to Jan, which Jan took as a caring gesture.

"Thanks," Jan replied.

"Don't thank me," Bronson told him. "I don't want you making me sick."

Lewis John Carlino, who remains disappointed by how his original concept for the film was altered, wasn't impressed by Jan's performance, which Jan himself later described as "wooden," an assessment Jan attributed to the monotonous pace that Winner, who was fond of shooting one line of dialogue at a time instead of entire scenes, brought to his direction of the film. "I thought that Jan brought the right physicality to the role of Steve but that his performance lacked dimensionality and came across flat," says Carlino, who responded much more favorably to Ben Foster's portrayal of Steve McKenna in the 2011 remake, which received a lukewarm commercial and critical reception. "I thought Jan gave very little to the role, though Michael Winner wasn't my favorite director and was someone who seemed to direct entirely for effect."

The production spent two months filming in Los Angeles and then spent three weeks in Naples, Italy, where Jan found female companionship but otherwise remained clean and sober. "Jan liked the ladies but had trouble with some women in Italy," says Kahana. "He was starting to act crazy, though he was straight during filming. I saw him go crazy, and I saw him starting to go down, which was around the time he started fighting with Bonnie, after we did *The Mechanic*. I think that's when the dope and drinking took complete hold of him."

The Mechanic was released in the United States in November 1972 and posted respectable but unspectacular grosses. Like so many of Bronson's films, *The Mechanic* did much stronger business in the international markets and found its largest audience in its long afterlife—on cable and video. The film, like Jan and the now well-worn Steve McKenna archetype he introduced, has found a minor rung within the pop culture lexicon.

7
The Star Chamber

After finishing work on *The Mechanic*, Jan barely had a week to relax before he had to begin training for the title role in his next film, *The World's Greatest Athlete*, a Disney spoof. *The World's Greatest Athlete* is a comedic reworking of *Tarzan*, and its box office success provided—much more than Jan's positive showings in *Going Home* and *Tribes* did—the most concrete foundation for Hollywood's belief in the inevitability of Jan's stardom.

The World's Greatest Athlete made Jan a sex symbol—he received upward of 5,000 fan letters a week following the film's February 1973 theatrical release, from girls and young women, many of whom are now grandmothers, many of whom remain loyal to him, and also undecided, in terms of whether they want to mother or make love to him, all of them convinced, still, that they could change him and make him well, if only they could get their hands on him. There were babies, children, boys and girls named Jan, whom he is undeniably responsible for.

Jan received second billing in the film to Tim Conway, and to the Disney banner, whose presence, throughout the 1970s, ensured a modest audience but scarcely anything more. This was a comedy, and Jan couldn't do comedy, as a fact and a rule, though the film would've been impossible unless Jan was able to pull off the illusion suggested by the title.

Jan ended up working much harder, physically, here than he did on any other project in his career, which is completely overshadowed by the embarrassing, inane dialogue and situations he was shackled to throughout filming and still has to live with. This is the film he's probably most remembered for.

Jan spent two months, prior to the start of filming in April 1972, training almost daily with Bill Toomey, the 1968 Olympic decathlon champion, in all aspects of track and field —high jumping, hurdling, long jumping, pole vaulting. The strain of this scared Jan off booze and pot until the end of filming, though he had little stamina, which wasn't really required, thanks to canny editing.

Like Bronson, who was built like a tank but was a chain smoker, Jan was able to go hard in thirty, forty second bursts, and then he ran out of gas. He aged, after forty, much more severely than did Bronson—even the Bronson who died of Alzheimer's-related pneumonia in 2003.

Other than the showcasing of Jan's beautiful body and smile, and the excitement and fandom that was built out of this, Jan's role in *The World's Greatest Athlete* is entirely thankless. The character of Nanu, Jan's version of Tarzan, is entirely reactionary, a pincushion, at the mercy of the barrage of cardboard buffoonery that all Disney stars endured in the 1970s. This era in the history of Disney's film division is regarded, rightfully so, as the most creatively dead and maudlin in the company's history, and the sight of bare

Jan running alongside a cheetah is one of the enduring emblems of this sad chapter. Among so many other titles Jan holds, he is a Disney star.

The film opens with Nanu living in the African region of Zambia, where he's discovered by two bumbling college coaches, played by Conway and John Amos, who see glorious possibilities in Nanu, as a track and field star, after they see Nanu outrun a cheetah. After navigating, and lying, through tribal politics, the coaches are able to coerce Nanu to return with them to the United States, where he is enrolled at Merrivale College and immediately thrown into the ultra-competitive environment of NCAA athletics.

Looking the part: *The World's Greatest Athlete* (1973).

There's a love interest—Jane Douglas, played by Dayle Haddon—and a villain, a rival for Jane's affections, who attempts to thwart Nanu's progress—

in athletics and with Jane—by convincing Nanu's godfather, the witch doctor Gazenga, played by Roscoe Lee Browne, that Nanu is being exploited. The same could have been said about Jan.

The film was shot primarily in Stockton, California—at San Joaquin Delta College and University of the Pacific—with Caswell Memorial State Park in Ripon, California doubling for the African jungle. Besides the departure of actor Godfrey Cambridge, who was replaced by Amos, after Cambridge collapsed a week into the filming, it was a benign, pleasant shoot, other than the moment when Jan almost had his throat ripped out by a Bengal tiger.

Tigers are not supposed to be native to Africa, a point the film deflects by having Nanu explain that Harri, AKA Harry, his beloved tiger, emigrated from India to Africa when he was a cub. Never mind. The more important point is that tigers on film sets are supposed to be, and usually are, carefully contained and isolated—and distracted—at all times, which is why tamers wave objects in front of them. These animals only really want to eat you.

Somehow, someway, Jan ended up alone with the tiger on the lake used for the filming, during the filming of a scene in which Jan and Harri are on a rowing boat. When Jan reached for an oar, the tiger leaped on him and put its mouth on Jan's throat, which elicited panic from the trainer, who was on the shore and started waving chickens' necks to try and get the tiger's attention. Jan resolved the crisis himself; he smacked the tiger on its nose with the oar, and the tiger immediately withdrew, with a surprised look on its face.

Danny Goldman, who had worked with and befriended Jan on *Tribes*, plays Nanu's conniving, nerdy rival in the film and saw in Jan, during the filming of *The World's Greatest Athlete*, someone who was being numbed by his exposure to the first wave of fame and near stardom. "We had become friends on *Tribes*, and Jan remembered that when we did *The World's Greatest Athlete*, and he recalled the time we had spent together at the army post, but he had also clearly changed," says Goldman. "He was friendly during the filming, but it also seemed to me that he was under the influence of drugs."

The World's Greatest Athlete grossed more than $20 million theatrically in North America, making it one of the ten highest-grossing films of the year and the highest-grossing film of Jan's career, not including the Burt Reynolds vehicle *Hooper* (1978), whose success had nothing to do with Jan.

The combination of *The Mechanic* and *The World's Greatest Athlete* turned out to be the most commercially-successful period of Jan's film career, which never soared beyond this point, in terms of Jan's bankability. This was—in terms of the idea that Jan was going to become a superstar—not a beginning, a launching point, but a prelude to obscurity. This was the peak.

In August 1972, Bonnie and Jan discovered that Bonnie was pregnant again.

Jan reacted joyously to the news, the excitement tempered only by the prior miscarriage. In the midst of this, Jan started work on the melodramatic made-for-television film *Sandcastles*, a fantasy romance that aired on CBS in October 1972.

Sandcastles, which was directed by Ted Post, a mentor of Clint Eastwood, was filmed in twelve days, at the CBS Studio Center, and on location in Malibu, which was now firmly entrenched as Jan's home turf.

Sandcastles, which was shot on videotape then transferred to 35MM, reunited Jan with Bonnie Bedelia, Jan's costar in the 1969 *Bonanza* episode "The Unwanted," and once again they were paired as doomed young would-be lovers. Bedelia's character in the film, Jenna, is a dreamily romantic orchestral musician, living in Los Angeles, who endlessly fantasizes about an angelic-looking blonde man, whom she believes is her true love.

This man is an invention of hers, but he really exists, in the form of Jan's character, Michael, a drifter who roams the coast, taking odd jobs. As the film opens, Michael is living near the beach, near San Francisco, where he has befriended a beachfront restaurant owner, Alexis, played by Herschel Bernardi, who looks at Michael as the son he never had.

When Alexis gives Michael $20,000 to deposit at the bank for him, Michael decides to split with the money but changes his mind and decides to return. While hitchhiking with a drunk driver, a car accident ensues. Finally, Bedelia and Jan are joined, when Jenna, who happens to be on her way to San Francisco, drives past the crash site. She finds a dying Michael and holds him in her arms until an ambulance arrives. Finally, the relationship between Jenna and Michael begins, with Michael appearing now in ghost form.

Ultimately, the film belongs to Bernardi, who was a semi-star of the sixties and seventies, usually in cop or gangster roles. As Michael's father figure, he displays a palpable sense of anger and loss, the only moments when the film makes the transition from melodrama to tragedy.

The most poignant aspect of Jan's work in *Sandcastles* is how emblematic the film is of the different shades of Jan's appearance throughout the 1970s—these were the dying days of Jan's blonde hippie look—and how closely the film's most haunting visual—the ocean breakers crashing against Michael's last sandcastle—matches the impact that Jan had on all those around him.

8
The Graduate

In November 1972, around the time of *The Mechanic*'s theatrical release, Jan, who was nearly ten years removed from Hanford High, played his last teenager on camera, when he appeared as a teenage gymnast on an episode of the television series *Marcus Welby, M.D.*.

In the episode, entitled "Catch a Ring That Isn't There," (February 6, 1973) Jan's character, Ritchie Manning, is a teenage alcoholic who experiences continual blackouts. This is one of the symptoms of alcohol abuse described to Ritchie by kindly Dr. Welby, along with liver damage and stomach poisoning, which Jan himself experienced—along with brain damage, failing teeth, impotence, paralysis, not to mention the millions of dollars in lost earnings and savings his drinking and using cost him, which is not an exaggeration.

Jan was twenty-eight when he played Ritchie, and he was an expectant father, a role Jan embraced and fulfilled wholeheartedly. Terrified of the possibility of a second miscarriage, Jan took every precaution with Bonnie: they attended birthing classes, and Jan monitored her diet closely, Jan intending to deliver the baby himself, through natural childbirth, in Malibu.

Film offers trickled in for Jan throughout the fall of 1972, prior to the downpour that arrived in the spring of 1973, in the wake of *The World's Greatest Athlete*'s release. However, film roles of a serious caliber skidded by Jan throughout the 1970s, slipping away, like butterflies do, before Jan could close his hands around them, and these missed opportunities accumulated throughout the decade, and then they became rarer and rarer, and then they stopped.

In October 1972, Jan was briefly attached to *Cruising*, a film adaptation of Gerald Walker's controversial 1970 novel, a psychological thriller about a New York cop who goes undercover, immersing himself in New York's gay and S&M community, to find a serial killer who is targeting homosexuals. Jeff Bridges, Jan's rival for several film roles throughout the 1970s, was attached to play the cop, Steve Burns, in the film, which was to have been directed by Andy Warhol associate Paul Morrissey, an edgy, underground filmmaker.

Jan was supposed to play Stuart Richards, a prime suspect in the killings, which would've allowed for an interesting commentary on Jan's own bisexual appeal, which was never fully exploited on camera, other than in the sleazy magazine pictorials of Jan's body that continued to follow him toward the end of his twenties and impending fatherhood.

Cruising didn't go into production until July 1979, with William Friedkin as director, Al Pacino in the role of Steve Burns, and Richard Cox taking over from Jan, whose film career was, by that time, basically over. Released in February 1980, the film was a commercial and critical disappointment, the latter much more damaging than the former, and brought little attention to Cox, a Broadway actor whose subsequent, largely unheralded, career has played out, fairly anonymously, in episodic television. This was, like the role in *Chisum*, probably not much of a loss for Jan.

Jan found his risk in March 1973, after returning from Europe, where he'd been sent on a promotional tour for *The World's Greatest Athlete*, which performed even better overseas than it did in the United States, to the point where Jan received an award in Germany—it was for Star of the Year, World Film Favorite, something silly.

When Jan read the script for *Buster and Billie*, a teenage love story that develops into a tragedy, set in 1948 Georgia, the character of Buster Lane, the film's protagonist, excited him so much that he knew he had to play the role.

Jan was hot at this moment and was flooded with offers; he turned down three of them in favor of *Buster and Billie*, which was written by neophyte Ron Turbeville, a native of Florence, South Carolina, who based the characters in his script on the people he knew in high school, specifically an abused, shy girl, who was known as the town tramp and was considered an easy "gang-bang" sexual target by Turbeville's male colleagues.

Billie's rape and murder in the film, and the revenge that Buster takes, was not based on Turbeville's personal story but another boy Turbeville had grown up with in South Carolina, who—like what happens to Buster in the film—was jailed for killing several of the perpetrators and then, in a grand existential gesture, visited the girl's grave after he made bail, where he laid down the flowers he'd ripped from various gardens.

Turbeville felt that girls like Billie were a staple of American high schools, and that this would make an intriguing subject, as did Jan, who knew of (which isn't the same as knowing) girls like Billie, the girls who believed they had to use sex to get attention.

Jan had also hung around with guys in Hanford who were comparable with Buster's friends in the story. Although Jan's teenage persona was much different from that of Buster Lane, who is Mr. Popularity at his high school, no one outside of Hanford would've believed that.

Buster and Billie was the most personal film in Jan's career; whereas *Tribes* captured Jan's undistinguished military career, *Buster and Billie* was about Hanford, his hometown, which Jan stayed in touch with throughout the 1970s. He visited Doris and Lloyd regularly, whenever he wasn't on location, and Jan liked to revisit the landmarks, when his rising fame didn't make this too difficult.

By the early seventies, with his acting career well-known all over Hanford, Jan's arrivals made news; there were no parades when he arrived in town, but there was subtle fanfare, and when he'd go to the Me-N-Ed's for a beer, wearing dark glasses, all of the kids in town saw him. "The guys and I saw Jan in the early 1970s, and we went surfing a few times," recalls Charlie Oncea. "We went to see Jan at his house in Malibu, after his baby was born. He lamented not being able to go home as much and not being able to go surfing with us anymore, like the old days. I didn't see him again after that."

Buster and Billie was a labor of love for Jan, who proved this time and time again between the project's start and finish. This was also the most collaborative experience in Jan's career; he met with Daniel Petrie—a careful, sensitive director, whom Jan bonded with more than any other filmmaker throughout his career—several times during the project's development and offered many suggestions, which included changing the project's title from *Black Creek Billie*, the original title, to *Buster and Billie.*

The only other actor mentioned for the role of Buster was Bruce Boxleitner, who did a screen test but fell away as soon as Jan expressed interest. *Buster and Billie* was Jan's first baby, and its completion coincided almost directly with the moment when Bonnie gave birth.

Jan, who ended up with a profit-sharing deal on *Buster and Billie*, said he would've done the film for nothing, and the $20,000 salary he accepted, which was about a tenth of what he could've found elsewhere, demonstrated his commitment to *Buster and Billie*, which began its production cycle with a budget of $300,000, the money provided by movie theater chain magnate Ted Mann.

Although *Buster and Billie* began filming as an independent production, Jan, Ted Mann, and Daniel Petrie had a tacit agreement with Columbia Pictures—and Columbia executive Peter Guber, who was named the studio's chief in 1973—that the studio would acquire the film for distribution, which is what happened. *Buster and Billie* marked the beginning of a multi-picture relationship between Jan and Columbia Pictures, and especially Guber, who was the first Hollywood power player to not only identify Jan as a potential superstar but also groom Jan for this.

In the first week of April, with Bonnie well into her third trimester, Jan and the rest of *Buster and Billie*'s small cast and crew traveled to Statesboro, Georgia, where the bulk of the film was shot. The filming began in the third week of April and was supposed to last thirty days, which would leave Jan, in theory, plenty of time to get back to California to be with Bonnie, who was due to give birth at the end of May, or in early June at the latest.

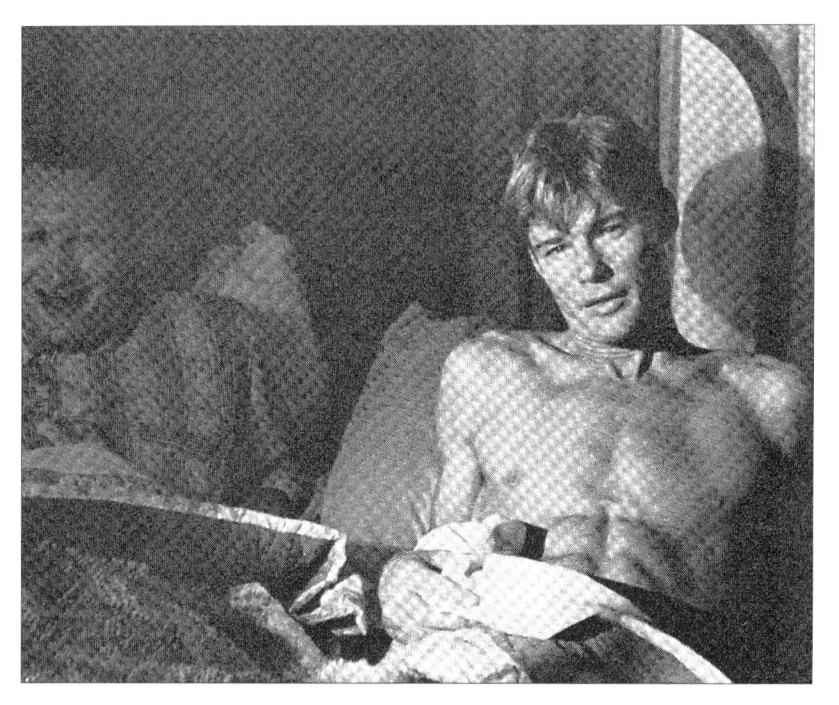

Jan received his best critical notices for his performance in the film *Buster and Billie* (1974).

Jan arrived in Statesboro with little more than a farmer's jacket, and the southern drawl he'd worked on in Malibu prior to flying to Georgia. There was no money for a wardrobe department; Jan and the rest of the cast found most of their characters' clothes from a local clothing store that was still in possession of dead stock from the 1940s, and the locals, several of whom were used to fill out scenes in the film, also provided the cars and trucks that appear in the film.

Jan moved into the Crossroads Motel, which he later referred to as the

"Crossroads Commune," a reference to the barren surroundings, where he was grouped with friend Robert Englund, who plays Buster's albino friend, Whitey, in the film, along with Englund's then girlfriend, actress and writer Janice Fischer. Then there was Joan Goodfellow, an exotic, unconventionally beautiful blonde bird, who was cast as Billie, Buster's doomed soul mate.

Although Buster is a high school senior, this does not represent another teenage role for Jan, though this distinction is only a technicality. The story takes place in 1948, post-World War II, and it is reasonable to assume that Jan and his classmates, who are future farmers, would've devoted their late teenage years to the war effort, thus putting them in their twenties.

This is, of course, semantics, and Jan does, unquestionably, appear too old and somewhat narcissistic in the film's opening scene, which shows Buster driving through the countryside, racing past a school bus, in his pickup, the latter characteristic more than partly attributable to cinematographer Mario Tosi, who became mesmerized by Jan during the filming and found it difficult to pull his camera away from Jan's eyes and face, which was apparent to Petrie when he first screened a rough cut of the film.

Jan was, typically, a slow starter, and after the first few days of filming, Jan slipped into this character, and through time, to deliver the most affecting and critically acclaimed performance in his career. A lot of the credit for this transformation goes to Goodfellow, a Method actress who had trained in New York, whose only previous screen appearance was a minor supporting role in the little-seen film *Lolly-Madonna XXX* (1973). They had immediate chemistry, and Goodfellow, following her character's trajectory, fell in love with Jan during the process.

This was simply a case of Goodfellow (or Joanie, as Jan liked to refer to her), who was about five years younger than Jan, taking her character, and her on screen relationship with Jan, a bit too seriously. Nothing happened between them during the filming. Jan did not get involved with his leading ladies, who were too far above his standards, which were much more easily met by extras, groupies, a waitress, wherever he was filming, away from

Bonnie. "Joan was a Method actress, and she really fell in love with Jan, even though she ended up marrying someone else from the location after we shot the film," recalls Englund. "When we weren't filming, it was just the four of us at the motel—me, Jan, my girlfriend, and Joan—and when Joan started going on about how much she loved Jan, Janice, my girlfriend at the time, kind of took her aside and said, 'Look, Jan's married, and he's going to have a baby, and you need to stop this.' Jan thought it was funny that Joan had a crush on him and treated her like she was his tomboy sister throughout the shoot."

Jan with his *Buster and Billie* costar, Joan Goodfellow.

Early in the filming schedule, Jan and Daniel Petrie were in the pool hall featured in the film, where they met Daniel Faircloth, a local raconteur and singer, a real character, who owned a dilapidated, legendary mansion in the area that became a hideaway for various Country & Western musicians, and for Jan, who gravitated toward this group and made several visits to Faircloth's mansion throughout the seventies and eighties. Goodfellow fell in love with Faircloth during the filming and married him immediately after the production ended.

The scenes in the film between Goodfellow and Jan are heartbreaking and insightful, particularly as Buster discovers, and unravels, the reasons for Billie's promiscuous behavior, which Buster convinces her she doesn't need to continue. There is a moment of near greatness for Jan in the film, in the scene where Buster, ignoring the feelings of everyone else in the town, takes Billie to church in his pickup truck, which is the final and not so subtle step along her path to redemption.

As Goodfellow projected some of her character's feelings toward Jan, Jan behaved like Buster off camera, in terms of the antics he pulled on location. "Jan would commandeer the prop cars, and then he'd drive to the state line to get some tequila, which he loved," recalls Englund. "He brought it back to us—me, Janice, Joan—and we'd have tequila and orange juice on the rocks. The four of us would also sneak off to Savannah some nights, and we'd roam through black neighborhoods, and we'd walk past all of these creepy, dirty mansion squares, which were straight out of *Midnight in the Garden of Good and Evil*. We talked about buying some of the old mansions."

Jan made film history in *Buster and Billie*, not with his performance, acclaimed as it was, but with the frontal nudity he displayed during the film's skinny dipping scene, the first time any actor had done this in a studio feature.

Statesboro, Georgia is part of the Bible Belt, which was apparent to the cast and crew when they were shooting a scene at a local farm and were approached by a farmer in a pickup trick, who was outraged, believing that *Buster and Billie* was "one of those Triple X sex movies," which was the rumor that circulated throughout the town. He was prepared to drive the cast and crew away, by force, until Petrie stepped in and calmed the man down by letting him look at the shooting script.

The skinny dipping scene between Goodfellow and Jan was filmed in a mill pond, which was located on a property that was owned by a local preacher. In order to get the shot of Goodfellow and Jan swinging out on a rope, naked, Petrie and the crew had to find a way to keep the preacher and his family out of sight. When the preacher and his family went inside, Goodfellow and Jan did the scene and then were joined in the water by the crew.

Jan generated attention in Georgia all by himself, and this represented, almost seven years into his acting career, the accumulation of *Tribes*, *The Mechanic*, and *The World's Greatest Athlete*, along with the magazine appearances. While Jan and Robert Englund were filming a beach scene on Jekyll Island, there were lots of girls watching. "They obviously weren't watching me, with my albino makeup and hairpiece," says Englund, who made his film debut with *Buster and Billie* and achieved his greatest fame with his portrayal of killer Freddy Krueger in the successful *Nightmare on Elm Street* film series. "Jan was one of the hottest young actors around at that moment. You could feel it."

Jan loved being in Statesboro during the filming, despite its limitations and his worries about Bonnie, whom he spoke to every day. The character, the subject matter, and the town reinvigorated Jan's small town sensibilities and values, which he demonstrated during the filming of the swing dancing scene, which was shot on a cold and rainy night, with a few dozen locals in Bolo ties and dresses serving as extras. When Jan sensed that the locals, who were freezing, were being neglected, he insisted that a restaurant be opened up in town, and he had hot chocolate and soup brought in for everyone. He cared.

The last day of filming was on May 18, 1973, the day before Jan's first and only child was born without him being there. On that day, in the afternoon, Jan, who was set to leave Georgia either that night or the following morning, called home to Malibu, which was when he found out that Bonnie had gone into labor and was taken to Santa Monica Hospital. The production scrambled to get Jan on a plane, so he could join Bonnie in time for the delivery. When Jan arrived at the hospital, on May 19, 1973, his daughter, Amber Springbird Vincent, was four hours old.

Although many critics objected to *Buster and Billie*'s violent ending—which is largely faithful to the real-life story—when the film was released in August 1974, Jan's performance drew modest praise, with the influential film critic Roger Ebert of the *Chicago Sun-Times* singling out the "fine performances" by Goodfellow and Jan in his three-star review.

Ted Mann, the film's backer, sold the distribution rights to *Buster and*

Billie to Columbia Pictures for $650,000, bringing Mann a tidy profit, which is what Columbia also reaped from the film. Studio head Peter Guber used the film, and Jan's performance, as the basis for his plan to groom Jan for stardom. This was an experiment that lasted until the spring of 1975, when Guber left his post at Columbia to go solo, a development that left Jan stranded.

Joan Goodfellow, who was so great in the film, received glowing reviews herself, which were also accompanied by the faintest whispers of a possible Oscar nomination. However, like Catherine Burns, the beautifully misshapen actress from the film *Last Summer* (1969), whose unforgettable, Oscar-nominated performance in that film was greeted by a chorus of ignorance in Hollywood, utter silence, nothing much happened for Goodfellow after this.

That she holds bitterness against Hollywood for failing, criminally so, to appreciate her rare talent and strange beauty is understandable. That she now feels disgust at the very mention of Jan's name is harder to understand, since they had gotten along so well in Georgia and continued to see each other, pleasantly so, around Malibu, where Goodfellow moved after *Buster and Billie* and her impulsive marriage to Daniel Faircloth, which ended after less than a year.

While Jan received the full Hollywood treatment, Goodfellow spent the next decade working, fairly steadily but without appreciation, mostly in television, appearing in several made-for-television films, with occasional supporting roles in minor features—nothing that provided an adequate showcase in which her amazing talent could flash. She just faded away.

Goodfellow gave up acting in 1986, after toiling for several months as a standby performer—which isn't the same as being an understudy—in the original Broadway production of *Biloxi Blues*. She moved back to her hometown of Wilmington, Delaware, near her mother, and looked for a much less punishing occupation, which turned out to be secretarial work.

The success of *The Mechanic* and *The World's Greatest Athlete* almost freed Jan from the bonds of television but not quite.

In July 1973, Jan took Bonnie and baby Amber with him—in the camper they used to travel to filming locations on the West Coast—to the rugged terrain of Mount Hood, Oregon, where Jan spent three weeks filming *Deliver Us from Evil* (1973), a compact, tense made-for-television film that aired on ABC in September 1973, kicking off the network's 1973-1974 Movie-of-the-Week season.

Jan is joined in the film by a gallery of memorable old faces—Charles Aidman, Jim Davis, Bradford Dillman, George Kennedy, Jack Weston—in this story of six male hikers who discover a downed skyjacker who is carrying $600,000 from his latest score. They kill the man and take the money, and then they end up turning on each other throughout the rest of the film. Jan's character, Nick Fleming, is the son of Aidman's character and ends up as the film's lone voice of reason.

In September, Jan returned to the Universal lot to film an episode of the short-lived crime drama television series *Toma*, entitled "Blockhouse Breakdown," (November 8, 1973) with Jan cast as a sniper, who picks off civilians from the top of an office building. This was the last villainous role Jan played throughout the decade.

Jan then played another sniper, the lawful kind, in an episode of the television series *Police Story*, entitled "Line of Fire," (December 18, 1973) with Jan appearing as a would-be sniper who joins the SWAT unit in Los Angeles, where he's tutored by the squad's coldblooded leader, who is played by Alex Cord, Jan's later costar on *Airwolf*. "I liked Jan immediately when we filmed the *Police Story* episode," says Cord, who did not see Jan again until they reunited on *Airwolf*. "With a *Police Story* episode, there was no time for standing around; you showed up each day and knew your lines and what to do. Jan was gifted; he wasn't, obviously, a skilled actor like a Christopher Plummer, but he had great natural ability and reminded me of [Marlon] Brando and [Al] Pacino, in terms of Jan's ability to grasp material and grasp the scene he was working on."

Jan also reminded Cord—both during the filming of the *Police Story* episode and during the *Airwolf* years—of Cord's own son, Damien Zachary Cord, who was four when the episode was filmed and died of a heroin overdose in 1995. "Our dressing rooms were very close together when we filmed the *Police Story* episode, and we talked a lot, and Jan reminded me a lot of my son—both then and when we worked on *Airwolf*, when Jan's addictions took over," says Cord. "Jan, like my son, was handsome and had magnetism, and I don't think Jan, like my son, did especially well in school. Jan and my son got along very well. Jan was confident when I first met him; he felt very deeply, as an actor, and he had a great sense of humor and a strong sense of himself when he was in front of the camera. When we did *Airwolf*, Jan reminded me of my son again, because of Jan's problems."

Jan did another episode of *Police Story* in 1975, the only television appearance he made between the beginning of 1974 and the end of 1979. He did not return to television in the 1980s; he crawled back to it.

Part Three

Easy to Steer

1974-1983

"Directing him was like driving a shiny red Corvette convertible."

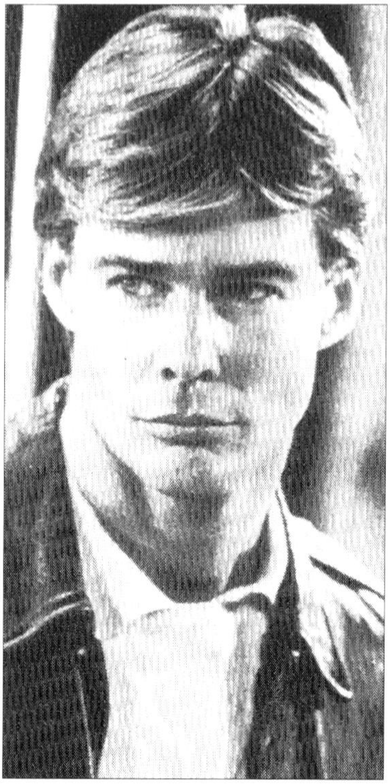

1
The Prodigy

For Jan to have attained the major film stardom that was predicted for him, he needed either a blockbuster commercial success to call his own or a critical breakthrough with an A-list director.

By 1974, the year Jan turned thirty, his profile was too high for him to claim the element of surprise in this quest, which soon became a full-blown experiment. He could not follow the paths taken by Harrison Ford, Tom Selleck, and Sylvester Stallone, three future stars, all around Jan's age, all practically invisible at this point, their anonymity giving them the appearance of novelty, making it appear as if they were overnight successes whose eventual rise to stardom, after a decade of struggle for each of them, took place in a single leap. No one remembers Ford—Jan's costar in *Journey to Shiloh*—before *Star Wars* (1977), or Selleck before the television series *Magnum, P.I.*, or Stallone before *Rocky* (1976).

Jeff Bridges, who is five years younger than Jan, received his second Oscar nomination—the first coming for *The Last Picture Show* (1971)—for the film *Thunderbolt and Lightfoot* (1974), a Clint Eastwood vehicle, in which Bridges' kooky, spirited performance managed to even coax a smile out of the normally taciturn Eastwood, whose screen persona lightened up considerably after his teaming with Bridges.

The themes and worlds of *The Last Picture Show*—a drama about small town decay—and *Thunderbolt and Lightfoot*—which is a meditation on male camaraderie and the decline of American traditions disguised as a buddy road film—are not that far removed from Jan's own experiences.

Jan could've easily connected with Duane Jackson, Bridges' character in *The Last Picture Show*; Duane is a recent high school graduate who leaves his hometown to go off, blindly, and enter the Korean war, recalling Jan's life in Hanford and his fears about being sent to Vietnam.

The role of Lightfoot was certainly written in Jan's rhythm—Bridges' Lightfoot is a young car thief, when he befriends Clint's Thunderbolt, a bank robber, who leads the kid on a lunatic odyssey to recover the hidden proceeds of Thunderbolt's previous robbery, pursued by Thunderbolt's former partners, one of whom ends up kicking Lightfoot in the head, which eventually kills him.

The characters of Duane and Lightfoot—as well as the direction of *The Last Picture Show*'s Peter Bogdanovich and *Thunderbolt and Lightfoot*'s Michael Cimino—might have revealed the extent of the versatility, the potential for expansion, in Jan's acting repertoire, which was not severely tested in Jan's effective but one-note performances in *Buster and Billie* and *Tribes*.

Jan at home with Amber.

Jan, as he reached the end of his twenties, was clearly too old to continue playing The Kid, not because of his appearance, which would've allowed this to continue up until his late thirties, but because of what was developing in his eyes and heart.

He would've found it very difficult, for example, to film a scene in *Thun-*

derbolt and Lightfoot in which Lightfoot and Thunderbolt escort two willing young women back to their motel for sex, which the girls expect them to pay for. Thunderbolt isn't bothered by this, but Lightfoot is outraged at the thought of paying for sex; he believes that if sex isn't free, it is immoral.

The new Jan agreed with Thunderbolt; he enjoyed the casual nature of the sexual activities he engaged in throughout this period, which fostered the emotional detachment he relied on to keep his mind off of Bonnie, and off of the shy boy he was in Hanford, who would've shared Lightfoot's outrage—as the Jan from four or five years earlier, around the time of *Tribes*, also would have. The loss of his romantic, small town idealism, which corrupted his soul, was the first byproduct, casualty, of his drinking.

Legend has it that Jan was considered for the role of oceanographer Matt Hooper in the film *Jaws* (1975), which was all that this rumor turned out to be. Jan never met with *Jaws* director Steven Spielberg, nor the producers, and he never did a screen test. Jan never progressed to the semi-final stage, with Bridges and Timothy Bottoms and several others, all of whom lost out to Richard Dreyfuss, who had been an early candidate for the Steve McKenna role in *The Mechanic*.

Jan was, during this period, almost exclusively tied to Columbia Pictures, who distributed five of Jan's films between 1974 and 1975. The only other outside projects Jan worked on during this period were the 1975 *Police Story* episode, entitled "Incident in the Kill Zone," (January 7, 1975) Jan's last television appearance in the 1970s, which was filmed in the fall of 1974, and the action film *Vigilante Force* (1976), which was filmed in 1975.

Jan was given a choice parking space on the Columbia lot, where most of Jan's press obligations were fulfilled; the interviews took place in the Columbia offices, Jan flocked by studio photographers, as he patiently and thoughtfully answered the reporters' questions, often holding a bottle of Heineken, his favorite beer, which he liked to back the tequila with.

The first project that Columbia tried to shuttle Jan into was originally titled *Street Fighter*, a depression-era action-drama about a mysterious stranger who arrives in Louisiana, where he finds fortune in the underground world of bare-knuckle matches.

Producer Lawrence Gordon, who later produced *Hooper*, was based at Columbia at the time and controlled the script, which was co-written by action auteur Walter Hill, who made his directorial debut with the film *Hard Times* (1975), the title that *Street Fighter* had morphed into when filming began in the fall of 1974.

It was Hill's original intention to cast a younger actor in the role of the fighter, Chaney, with Jan at the top of the list. However, Charles Bronson ended up taking the part and delivered, arguably, the definitive starring performance of his career.

The first film Jan started work on for Columbia, following *Buster and Billie*, was *Bite the Bullet* (1975), which began filming in April 1974. *Bite the Bullet*, which was directed and written by Richard Brooks, the most distinguished, prestigious filmmaker Jan ever worked with, marked Jan's last appearance in the western genre, whose traditions had entered the realm of anachronism, both in 1906, when *Bite the Bullet* is set, and certainly in the present, in Hollywood.

In *Bite the Bullet,* which sentimentalizes the dying western landscape through the lives of the participants in a grueling 700 mile cross-country horseback endurance race, the advancement of civilization is represented by the appearance of a newspaper reporter on a motorbike. There are also the trains—the trains that bring the contestants to the starting line of the $2,000 challenge, and the trains that the race's sponsor uses to monitor the contestants' progress.

In Hollywood, by 1974, this shift was represented by the advance of the "street western," the modern action movie paradigm, which began with the cop and private eye thrillers that Bronson, Eastwood, McQueen, Reynolds, and even Wayne had settled into, Wayne the most awkwardly.

Bite the Bullet once again placed Jan within the student-teacher model, the mentor played this time by Gene Hackman, who was, among all of the legends Jan worked with, the least protective of his stardom, which was tied to Hackman's essential identity as a character actor, which he never stopped being, not even by the time he was proclaimed, in many quarters, the second greatest screen actor of his generation, behind only Jack Nicholson.

Between his Oscar win for *The French Connection* (1971) and his appearance in *Bite the Bullet*, Hackman had enjoyed a big commercial success with *The Poseidon Adventure* (1972) and found one of his most brilliant characterizations in *The Conversation* (1973), while his salary inched upward toward the $1 million level, a mark he reached for the first time with *Lucky Lady* (1975), the lackluster, prohibition-era comedy Hackman filmed after *Bite the Bullet*.

Because Hackman was unburdened by early fame, as well as handsomeness, he was the least self-aware of the stars Jan worked with in the seventies, so there were none of the territorial rights issues that Jan had faced with Bronson, Mitchum, and Wayne. Hackman occupied much less space; his only demand was that his colleagues behave in a professional manner, starting with the director, and Jan—who received fifth billing in *Bite the Bullet*, beneath James Coburn and Ben Johnson—did nothing to violate this rule and raise Hackman's legendary temper during the filming, which took place on location in Nevada and New Mexico between the first week of April and the end of June.

Carbo, Jan's character, is, as the name implies, the cocky, volatile punk in the race, who represents the exact counterpoint to the values of Hackman's Sam Clayton; their antagonistic relationship embodies the film's secondary subject: the film's great love and respect for horses.

Clayton, a former Rough Rider under Teddy Roosevelt, loves these animals more than he does his best friend and partner, played by Coburn, whom he's willing to sacrifice if it will allow him to win the contest. Carbo, who directs his rage through his abuse of horses, offends Sam, first by punching a donkey to the ground outside a boarding house, which earns him a beating. Later in the film, Sam strangles Carbo after Carbo gets mad at the horse belonging to Miss Jones, played by Candice Bergen, whom Carbo calls a whore. About Carbo it is said: "A boy looking for a reputation is the most dangerous thing alive."

A reputation is all Carbo is, and it's almost all fiction; Carbo—like the Schofield Kid character in Eastwood's *Unforgiven* (1992)—has never killed a living creature in his life, and when he does cross this threshold, for the first time, he knows there will never be a second time. The Schofield Kid undergoes this transformation after killing a man; Carbo's education comes after the horse he has whipped violently across the desert collapses and dies. Sam finds the corpse and orders Carbo to bury it, which Carbo does, under the supervision of a reporter from the *Western Press*, the newspaper sponsoring the contest.

Jan received his education from Brooks, who did not provide the actors with a completed shooting script during the production, which was how Brooks liked to work. Jan had seen an outline prior to the start of filming and, along with the rest of the cast, received daily "sides" on each day of filming, where he found his lines of dialogue for the next day's shooting. This was not the kind of structure Jan was equipped to excel within, but he did, relying on his "acting by feel" approach, turning in—alongside *Buster and Billie* and *Tribes*—one of his best performances, which has been completely ignored.

The flash of greatness Jan shows in *Bite the Bullet* is much more fleeting than the one in *Buster and Billie*, in the scene where Buster gallantly escorts Billie, the town whore, from his pickup truck to the front of the church. The moment happens early in *Bite the Bullet*, when Carbo rides his horse into a boarding house saloon and tells the barmaid: "Whiskey for me and a beer for my horse."

Like the characters in the film, Brooks and Jan were both after triumph—the first for Jan and the last for the aging Brooks, who died in 1992, well before the film's rediscovery. This did not materialize until they were both dead, figuratively and literally, and certainly wasn't apparent upon the film's 1975 release, which was greeted by mixed reviews, with Vincent Canby of the *New York Times* placing *Bite the Bullet* among the worst films of 1975, while Roger Ebert praised the film as "a finely crafted, epic western," in his three-and-a-half star review.

Columbia Pictures dutifully mounted an Oscar campaign for *Bite the Bullet*, which carried a $4 million production cost, and this yielded two nominations, for Best Music and Best Sound. The film grossed a little over $10 million domestically, which made it—after the cost of promotion and the calculation of rentals—a break even result, financially, for the studio, as it was, momentum-wise, for Jan, whose flashy performance might as well have been innocuous.

On a personal level, baby Amber reached her first birthday during the filming of *Bite the Bullet*, and it was already obvious, before the bloom of her fair skin and the sprouting of her yellow hair, that she was the spitting image of Jan, whom she's now estranged from.

2
Confidence Man

The most ambitious film project Jan was attached to in the 1970s, besides *Cruising*, was *The Front Runner*, a proposed film adaptation of Patricia Neil Warren's 1974 novel of the same name, which tells the story of a gay track and field coach who falls in love with one of his male runners. Paul Newman, who optioned the novel after its publication, wanted to play Harlan Brown, the coach, and Jan was set to play Billy Sive, Brown's lover and protégé.

Like the Stuart Richards character in *Cruising*, the role of Billy Sive would've forced Jan to confront the gay identity that Jan's legion of gay followers had foisted, incorrectly, upon him. However, despite Newman's involvement and persistence, he was unable to convince United Artists, the studio Newman had a multi-picture deal with, to finance the project, unless Newman agreed to alter the project to allow the coach to go straight at the end of the film. Newman balked at this and let go of his option, which was then picked up by Frank Perry, an adventurous director, who was also unable to secure financing.

The next film Jan made for Columbia Pictures, following *Bite the Bullet*, was *White Line Fever*, an action film set against the backdrop of the CB radio/trucking culture that was so prevalent in American culture in the 1970s, in which *White Line Fever* serves as one of the most notable relics. *White Line Fever* turned into another one of Jan's "cult films," a film whose legacy would only be fully appreciated decades later, after Jan was long gone, although it was, by far, the most commercially-successful film Jan made for the studio.

White Line Fever was born out of an almost comical misunderstanding between Peter Guber and Jonathan Kaplan, *White Line Fever*'s director and co-writer, whose previous film, the urban exploitation—or "blaxploitation"—action film *Truck Turner* (1974), had earned a tidy profit for its distributor, American International Pictures, and brought Kaplan to the attention of Guber, who had only looked at the top of the page and assumed, not unreasonably so, that *Truck Turner* was a trucking film. "It [*Truck Turner*] was a minor success for AIP, a big hit in Chicago and Detroit, and when Peter saw the opening weekend numbers, he wanted to work with me," recalls Kaplan, who co-wrote the *White Line Fever* script with longtime collaborator Ken Friedman. "On the following Monday, Ken had written a treatment for a trucking western, which, of course, was nothing like *Truck Turner*, which was a blaxploitation film, whose only relationship with the trucking genre was its name. After all of that confusion was sorted out, Peter Guber had our treatment for *White Line Fever*, and then I met with Peter, and that's when I heard about Jan and how high Peter was on Jan and how he was convinced that Jan was going to become a major star. He was grooming Jan for stardom and wanted Jan in Columbia films."

Kaplan's initial meeting with Guber took place in the summer of 1974, prior to *Buster and Billie*'s release, and then Guber showed Kaplan, who was largely unaware of Jan's work, dailies of the film, in the aftermath of a discussion about developing *White Line Fever* as a starring vehicle for Jan. "I didn't know who Jan was at that point, but when Peter showed me a rough cut of *Buster and Billie*, I was very impressed," says Kaplan, who was the first director that Jan befriended. "I was twenty-five or twenty-six at this time, and the Jan I saw in *Buster and Billie*—and the Jan I worked with on the film—was very young," says Kaplan. "He was very simple and sweet, before he got on drugs, coke, which he was introduced to on our film by a stuntman he worked with. He had natural ability and presence, not just in terms of becoming a star but as an actor. I think he could've been a great actor."

The Jan that Kaplan met in Los Angeles—and in Tucson, Arizona, where the film was shot—was, according to Kaplan, a former Disney actor, referring to Jan's appearance in *The World's Greatest Athlete* but also to the Hanford upbringing that Kaplan —like almost everyone Jan worked with in his career—was unaware of. "Later on, I worked with Jodie Foster and Kurt Russell, former Disney actors, and everything was 'Sir' and 'Yes, sir,' and that's what Jan was like," says Kaplan. "I had to tell them to stop it, and it was the same with Jan, who was very deferential and lacked confidence."

White Line Fever's $1.4 million budget was largely financed by the adventurous but burly Hungarian-Canadian film producer John Kemeny and the consortium of real estate developers he brought together. Although Jan was granted few luxuries when he arrived in Tucson and checked into the local Hilton with the rest of the cast and crew, his movements were of great importance to the financiers, and especially the executives at Columbia Pictures, who wanted Jan, their new golden boy, to be handled with kid gloves at all times, which is not what Jan wanted at all.

Jan's character in the film, Carrol Jo Hummer, is a born trucker, and Jan, who had never encountered this breed in Hanford but greatly empathized with the plight of the truckers (the brutal driving schedules, the dangerous cargo, their pennies-on-the-dollar wages) he met in Tucson, wanted to acclimate himself to the physicality of this greatly undervalued profession, much to the dismay of the production team, and the studio. "Jan begged me to let him do his own stunts, to prove to the crew—and especially the stunt crew—that he was a man's man," says Kaplan. "He wanted to do all the physical stuff; he wanted to ride on the truck, on the box and the cab, and he did. One of the producers, Sheldon Schrager, was there, and he said to Jan, 'Jan, we can't put you in this kind of jeopardy,' but Jan didn't care. The insurance company had a fit over this, and when word got back to Columbia Pictures, they went crazy. Both Columbia and the insurance company put an end to the truck stunts."

Other than taking place inside the world of trucking, the elements of *White Line Fever* are similar to other revenge-driven action films from the time period, so many of which, like *White Line Fever*, found an enthusiastic reception within the drive-in and neighborhood movie house circuit.

Carrol Jo Hummer is a Vietnam War hero. Carrol wants to follow in the footsteps of his late father, a former trucker. He does this by purchasing a new truck and then going to work for the same shipping company his father worked for, a company that is now corrupt. When Carrol protests the company's hauling of contraband, he is blackballed, which prevents Carrol from finding work anywhere else. The shipping company is a front for a larger corporation, which is run by organized crime. When Carrol tries to organize the other drivers in Tucson to stand up to the evil corporation, he is beaten, cheated out of loads, and framed for murder. Then they attack his wife, Jerri, played by Kay Lenz, who is carrying their unborn child, which she loses.

Jan's insistence on getting his hands dirty during the filming might have been a hedge against dealing with the collaborative and creative aspects of the filming process he was still uncomfortable with, in terms of expressing his thoughts to a director, if he had any. "I think Jan's lack of confidence, which surprised me at first because of how talented he was, came from how he was marketed early in his career," says Kaplan. "He was marketed as a male model, and I think he went through an identity crisis and was never able to escape this and build his confidence, except for *White Line Fever*, which I think was the film in which he found his confidence. He didn't know how to trust his instincts, and he didn't know how to improvise, which is something I forced him to do in Tucson. Kay and the others weren't afraid to improvise or speak up, but Jan was reluctant. I said to him, 'You're really good, so just let go. You've got everything it takes to be a great actor.' I think he was a talented actor, blessed with natural gifts but surrounded by bad external forces. I also think he had bad management."

Kaplan wanted to make a Sam Peckinpah-type road western, and to help with this, he rounded out the cast with Peckinpah veterans R.G. Armstrong, L.Q. Jones, as well as Slim Pickens, who had grown up in Hanford, about a quarter of a century before Jan, and had been victimized by the same Drama teacher who told Jan he had no future as an actor. "They all gave Jan good advice and shared their experiences with Jan, who didn't do much drinking during the filming," says Kaplan. "Jan told me about his previous experiences working with John Wayne, whom he adored, and Mitchum, and also Bronson, which was an experience he described as being a real bummer for him. Jan heard Slim and the others talk about working with Peckinpah, and Jan talked about growing up in Hanford, and I think Jan was impressed by how Slim and the others were able to relax, have a good time but still do good work. Slim—and Sam Laws, who played Pops in the film and had been in *Truck Turner*—really encouraged and mentored Jan, and Slim told me that he thought that Jan had everything it took to become a big star."

As had happened during the making of *Buster and Billie*, Jan's performance developed over the six weeks of filming in Tucson, and Jan ended up being prouder of his intimate scenes with Kay Lenz than the physical requirements, although the film would've collapsed if Jan had been unable to drive and wield a shotgun simultaneously. "Jan started off wanting to impress us with his physicality and ended up impressing us the most with his scenes with Kay," says Kaplan. "He was most proud of his ability to deliver in the emotional and intimate scenes and to capture those emotions without dialogue. He had technique as an actor, and his star quality came from his own humility and his ability to project humility, which was his gift, beyond his looks—beyond the glorified model he was portrayed as in Hollywood."

There was drinking in Tucson, and Jan hooked up with a bit player in the film, habits that weren't at all deleterious to his performance or his relationships with the cast and crew. He ran into Lee Marvin, a Tucson native, at the local bar; Marvin, who may or may not have seen any of Jan's films, seconded Pickens' opinion of Jan's prospects. When Jan was given cocaine for the first time, which was given to him by a stuntman who doubled for him in the film, Jan reacted with a combination of bemusement and wonder; he shared the news of his discovery as if he'd been given a new toy. "He told Kay, and then he told me," says Kaplan. "The stunt coordinator gave it to Jan, and Jan became dependent on his stuntman for drugs from that point on. Jan told me it was the first time he'd tried it."

It would be irresponsible and unfair to name the human slime who introduced Jan to cocaine in Tucson, who is unnamed by the cast and crew, beyond the description of a stuntman who worked with Jan on the film and remained with Jan throughout the rest of the decade. If this description is accurate, the list is very short. In fact, there's no need for a list at all.

White Line Fever grossed nearly $15 million during its initial theatrical release in July 1975, a figure that does not tell the whole story, which continued to develop in offbeat locations across North America well past 1975, and on television, where the film's network premiere on ABC in 1977, during the 1977 World Series, drew massive ratings. By early 1976, it was estimated that the film had earned nearly $40 million. "Guber was thrilled with how the movie turned out," says Kaplan. "He later told me that *White Line Fever* was Columbia's most profitable movie for 1975."

Like the quick turnover between *The Mechanic* and *The World's Greatest*

Athlete, Jan had little time to recover from the making of *White Line Fever* before he had to start work on his next film, Columbia's *Baby Blue Marine*, which began filming in the first week of May 1975, in tiny McCloud, California, near Mount Shasta.

Jan returned home from Tucson, with his new confidence, which quickly took itself away.

3
Mistaken Identity

Baby Blue Marine returned Jan to wartime, to 1943, five years before the events of *Buster and Billie*, during World War II, his father's war.

Jan had always wondered how he would've performed under fire, both in Vietnam and World War II, and when he read the script for *Baby Blue Marine*, he felt fortunate for having scraped through basic training, not ending up like *Baby Blue Marine*'s protagonist, Marion, a dishonorably discharged Marine recruit, who is forced to wear a demeaning blue uniform—the costume attached to army rejects—when he is sent home. If Jan had ever been such a failure, a washout, he had, by the time he made *Baby Blue Marine*, long passed the point where he looked like a loser—the Jan Vincent from Fort Ord, Company D, First Battalion and Third Brigade.

The script was written by Stanford Whitmore, a veteran Hollywood writer, mostly from television, who based the story on his own experiences as a marine enlistee in 1943, when he witnessed a busload of marine rejects, dressed in the baby blue uniforms, and was haunted by the sight of their sadness and utter emasculation.

Producers Leonard Goldberg and Aaron Spelling, whose production company, Goldberg-Spelling Productions, was stationed on the Columbia lot, had bought the script in February 1975, and they turned it over to director John Hancock, a dramatist whose previous film, the sports drama *Bang the Drum Slowly* (1973), had earned widespread acclaim for Hancock's direction and the performance of a young Robert De Niro.

The conscientious objector: *Baby Blue Marine* (1976).

Hancock was a character-based, thoughtful filmmaker, not unlike Donald Petrie but more demanding and precise. Hancock wanted to cast Richard Thomas, who was then starring on the television series *The Waltons*, for the role of Marion and did not share Petrie's level of enthusiasm for Jan's abilities. "It was between Jan and Richard Thomas, and the studio wanted Jan, because they thought that Jan would be a bigger draw," says Hancock. "I met with Jan, and I liked him, though he had few suggestions when we talked about his character and the script. He was an actor; not a great actor but very attractive."

The collaborative relationship that existed between Jan and Petrie during the filming of *Buster and Billie* was contrasted by silence during the filming of *Baby Blue Marine*, in McCloud, California, doubling for Bidwell, the small Northern California community Marion enters after being assaulted in Los Angeles by an emotionally-scarred Marine Raider (played by a white-haired Richard Gere, in one of his earliest film appearances), who switches uniforms with Marion, which explains why the residents of Bidwell, reeling from the effects of the war, treat Marion like a hero.

Hancock, who was not aware of Jan's background, was satisfied with Jan's performance, rightfully so, but could not get past his nagging belief that Jan was both too old and too handsome to be believable as this loser vagabond. "I didn't think Jan was right for the part, because I didn't think it would be believable that Jan could not be successful as a marine," says Hancock. "Jan, himself, did not look like the washout he plays in the film; he looked like a successful marine. Jan was not at all a collaborator but an actor who simply knew his lines and worked hard. Jan was good looking, and he had some ability and a very sweet nature, but I felt that Jan—and I'm serious when I say this—needed acting lessons, and I think he would've benefitted greatly from this."

Jan, whose performance in *Baby Blue Marine* was cited by many of his later colleagues as his best film performance, does everything that's required in this performance, and the fact that he looks like he walked out of a recruitment poster does not detract from the character's sincerity, or Jan's, which began to leave him during the making of *Baby Blue Marine*. It is this transformation—Jan's not Marion's—that brings an additional level of context to the character and the film, a double meaning, which would not have existed with everyman Richard Thomas, if Hancock had gotten his way.

Jan bears no responsibility for the film's ultimate failure, the near miss that represented, on a personal level, the most heartbreaking disappointment in Jan's film career. This is entirely related to the film's awkward final act, the last thirty minutes or so, which overshadows the film's absorbing first hour.

Jan, and the film, can seemingly do no wrong up to this point, beginning with the moment when Marion, who intends to hitchhike back to his hometown of St. Louis, arrives in Bidwell, wearing the hero's uniform, and visits the local diner, where he meets Rose, played by Glynnis O'Connor, a young waitress who immediately falls in love with Marion, who represents the sum of all of her high school crushes.

The acting and direction are very assured here, and this generates a spell that continues through the predictable next section of the film, when Marion, the false war hero, is paraded in front of the townspeople, all of whom have been affected by the war and invest their feelings in, and through, Marion. Jan's approach is very subtle; he does not lie to these people, which would be cruel, so much as he stands still and lets them project their aspirations onto him. He listens, which was one of Jan's most overlooked gifts, so it appears that he is agreeing with the conclusions they've drawn about him, basely solely on his attire, instead of playing a cruel hoax. The only person Marion confides in is Rose, with whom Marion has a romantic interlude in a field of wildflowers.

This is enough. Unfortunately, there is more. A cancerous subplot enters the film, involving a nearby detention camp holding Japanese-Americans, three of whom escape, and so instead of the film ending with the resolution of Marion's deception, it ends with Marion and the escapees, whom he finds on the opposite side of a roaring river, a river Marion falls into after he is mistakenly shot by a crazed draftee, part of the posse out looking for the escapees. The Japanese-Americans pull Marion out of the water, and the final shot of the film shows Marion being recognized as a hero—the hero he never was before.

Like the ending of *Buster and Billie*, the ending of *Baby Blue Marine* represents, more or less, an accurate translation of the source material, and, also like the ending of *Buster and Billie*, the ending of *Baby Blue Marine* is incongruous with the rest of the film. "*Baby Blue Marine* ends on such a puzzling, inconsequential note that it's easy to forget how many good things came before," said Roger Ebert, in the first sentence of his review of the film, which represented the overall critical reaction to the film, which was mixed.

Columbia released *Baby Blue Marine* in May 1976, using the same approach they'd taken with *Buster and Billie*, marketing *Baby Blue Marine* as a love story, emphasizing Jan's name, which did not turn out to have nearly the value that the studio had envisioned, as was reflected in the film's miniscule grosses.

Baby Blue Marine was the last film of Jan's to be overseen by Peter Guber, who was long gone from his position as studio chief when the film was released. When Guber left Columbia, Jan lost his most influential supporter and the level of attention and caring that had been included in Jan's relationship with the studio. The new regime showed much less patience with Jan.

Jan's next film after B*aby Blue Marine, Vigilante Force*, began filming in the middle of June 1975, in and around Los Angeles. This was another rapid fire transition for Jan, his third film in less than six months, which was agreeable to Jan, who wanted respite from his relationship with Bonnie, which had grown tense and was on its last legs.

Conscious of how commercially-dicey *Baby Blue Marine* was going to be, Jan had signed on to *Vigilante Force* before the start of filming on *Baby Blue Marine*, sensing the need to insure the risk of *Baby Blue Marine* with what looked like a surefire box office hit, which was *Vigilante Force*'s only reason for being. This is the kind of cynical calculation that almost always turns back on itself, and everything about *Vigilante Force*, which ended up taking in less money than *Baby Blue Marine*, was decidedly retrograde.

Jan described *Vigilante Force* as "a brand new cowboy picture," Jan receiving second billing in the film to Kris Kristofferson, Jan playing a resident in a small California town, which is overrun with rowdy, violent behavior by nearby oil field workers. Jan's character, Ben Arnold, seeks help from Kristofferson, his Vietnam veteran brother, who recruits a team of mercenaries, Vietnam comrades, to pacify the oil field workers, which they succeed at with ruthless efficiency. Then Kristofferson and his army take control of the town for themselves and their illegal purposes, which forces Ben to turn against his brother.

Vigilante Force is an unsubtle satire, a minor allegory, of the post-Vietnam American way of life in the 1970s, in the guise of a fast-paced, exploitation picture. The mixture baffled the film's distributor, United Artists, which only gave *Vigilante Force* a limited release in September 1976, with predictably gloomy results.

The failures of *Baby Blue Marine* and *Vigilante Force* were not at all immediately apparent to Jan (who sprained his ankle in the last week of *Vigilante Force*'s filming while piggy-backing two-year-old Amber in the woods behind the Topanga Canyon house) when he decided to take a break, beginning in August 1975—a breather from his film career and marriage, which both collapsed in 1976.

4
Shadow of the Turkeys

Jan's separation from Bonnie, which unfolded in the spring of 1976 but wasn't announced until early 1977, didn't represent much of a change from the recent state of their marriage, which had, since Amber's birth, existed within the loose parameters of an open marriage.

This arrangement had been entirely Jan's idea, and they were his rules—for both of them to come and go as they wanted, to do whatever made them happy, to follow the stars. Jan felt he had earned this privilege by paying for Bonnie's life of pottery, sculpting, which was followed later by writing. All of these activities had served their primary purpose, which was to keep Bonnie busy and her eyes away from Jan's lifestyle. However, there was no career to be had for her in any of this.

The only hiccup in the otherwise peaceful, quick legal process was some minor wrangling over the marriage itself and just what had taken place in Mexico, during the filming of *Danger Island*, when Bonnie and Jan had exchanged their own vows. There was a brief spark of acrimony here when Jan's lawyer suggested that there had never been a marriage, but this was short-lived.

There had been a marriage by any definition, although the seemingly endless separation that followed—it was a long, winding road to divorce—did transport them back in time to the uncharted territory their relationship had originated from. They were meant to be together.

The duration of their separation—which lasted until April of 1984, when Bonnie filed for divorce—matched, almost exactly, the length of the marriage, which was effectively over the moment Bonnie moved out of the Topanga Canyon residence with Amber. This was a prelude to a long period—many years—in which they both held out hope for a reunion.

Bonnie, who has since remarried, moved to Sun Valley, Idaho, her current location, where she settled on a ranch property, with Amber, who visited Jan—who, unfailingly, supported this horse-rich lifestyle—on holidays, under the terms of a joint custody agreement that functioned fairly smoothly throughout Amber's adolescence.

Jan—who was, according to friends, devastated by the separation and lost without Bonnie—moved closer to the Malibu sand, living in a hillside house that he and several of his surfing buddies constructed in 1976, although Jan spent as much time in the back of his pickup truck during the aftermath of the separation, never far from the beach.

His real estate holdings were considerable. Besides this house and the Topanga Canyon residence, there was the land in Santa Barbara that he built a house on—this was the house he constructed out of the wood from a water tank. He owned a ten-acre spread in Encinal Canyon and a house in Orange County. This collection is now worth tens of millions of dollars. It's all long gone. Daryl Hannah, Jan's costar in the film *Hard Country* (1981), later bought the Encinal Canyon property, where she lived for many years.

Nothing that happened in Jan's professional life between 1976 and 1977 would lighten his mood. After the filming of *Vigilante Force*, and the six month sabbatical he'd taken afterward, Jan's next film project, his final obligation to Columbia Pictures, was *Shadow of the Hawk*, a project he signed up for in the fall of 1975, when he was basking in the afterglow of *White Line Fever*'s success.

Shadow of the Hawk, which began filming in March 1976, in Vancouver, British Columbia, Canada, would turn out to be not just a failure but the most obscure title in Jan's film career and certainly one of the most unusual projects to be released by a major studio in the 1970s, or any other period.

It never starts out this way, and *Shadow of the Hawk* was no different. When Columbia bought the script, which was written by Norman Thaddeus Vane, they saw exciting possibilities, a potentially entertaining and even enlightening film, in this story of a westernized young man, a half-Indian, who has found success in the white corporate world at the cost of his heritage, which he has rejected but is forced to revisit when his grandfather—a shaman the young man hasn't seen in many years—arrives at his doorstep and tricks the young man into taking him back to the reserve, where the young man has frightening mystical experiences that eventually compel him to join his grandfather on a tribal walk among evil spirits.

There would, of course, be the influence of special effects, and the script included a requisite love interest for the young man, Mike, who must reclaim his identity on this journey—this is the journey of a half-Indian who must evolve from callow white man to real human being, a theme that was later explored, much more convincingly and successfully, in the film *Thunderheart* (1992).

Everything about the packaging of *Shadow of the Hawk*'s elements represented business as usual in Hollywood; there was nothing, early on, to even hint at the obsolescence that now blankets the film, which has made only sporadic appearances on television over the years, mostly on the aboriginal channels. Columbia, still excited about Jan and wanting to repeat the success of *White Line Fever*, turned the project over to *White Line Fever*'s producer, John Kemeny, ignoring the frosty relationship that had existed between Jan and Kemeny in Tucson, as well as the contribution of Jonathan Kaplan, *White Line Fever*'s director, who was not consulted until it was too late.

Instead, Columbia hired Jack Smight, a prolific, matter-of-fact director from film and television, to direct the $1.8 million film, a sound choice that was driven by Smight's enthusiasm for the material and the box office success of his most recent film, *Airport 1975* (1974), which grossed nearly $50 million domestically against its $3 million budget. *Midway* (1976), the epic war film that Smight had filmed before joining *Shadow of the Hawk*, performed similarly well, with a much higher budget, when it was released in June 1976, just a month before *Shadow of the Hawk*'s doomed release.

There was a feeling of optimism when Smight—with whom Jan later worked on the film *Damnation Alley*, which was filmed in the summer of 1976—arrived in Vancouver in November 1975, and settled into the film's production office to begin the post-production process, which quickly bogged down, mainly due to script revisions, which saw a revolving door of writers come and go. The relationship between Kemeny and Smight, which was tense from the beginning, quickly worsened, resulting in Smight's departure.

Part Three: Easy to Steer 1974-1983

In January 1976, Daryl Duke, a Canadian director working in Hollywood, who had earned rave reviews for his brilliant character drama film *Payday* (1973), was announced as Smight's replacement. This did not hasten the completion of a shooting script. The script went through countless more revisions, while the production descended into chaos.

By the time Jan arrived in Vancouver, in the third week of February, Duke was still working on script rewrites and was eventually fired, less than a week before filming was set to begin. Duke was replaced by George McCowan, another Canadian director, whose bland name fit his dense, one-take approach, in a thankless career that was defined by such horrible circumstances, in which McCowan's role, his job with a capital J, was to get said film in the can and get the hell out of town. This is how everyone on the cast and crew felt about *Shadow of the Hawk*, which is what happens when a film has had its heart ripped out.

Besides the three directors, *Shadow of the Hawk* went through two art directors, two first assistant directors, three directors of photography, two script supervisors, and on and on. Marilyn Hassett, who had gained temporary fame for her performance in the tearjerker film *The Other Side of the Mountain* (1975), was cast as the female lead, Jan's love interest. She became ill and remained so throughout the filming, weakening an already tenuous subplot in the film. The great Chief Dan George, who plays Jan's grandfather, also became ill, restricting his movements and the amount of time he could work.

Jan could, by this point in his career, sense when a film was going in the right or wrong direction but did not know how to exercise his power, which was modest in stature but wielded enough influence, between 1975 and 1976, to force necessary changes. Power in Hollywood translates into capital, which is a resource, like momentum, that is never more potent than when it's gone. Jan did not spend a penny of this.

He began every film with high hopes, including *Shadow of the Hawk*, and when he saw things starting to erode, his response was to withdraw from rather than engage with the source of the problem, though he did not remain completely idle while *Shadow of the Hawk* was falling apart.

Desperate, Jan called Jonathan Kaplan, who had become a friend, from Vancouver and begged Kaplan to come to Vancouver and take over the film. "Jan called me, and he was very upset, because they'd fired the director, and he said it was a disaster," recalls Kaplan. "He said, 'You've got to come and help me; you've got to take over.' I told him I couldn't do it. I think there was arrogance with that project; the studio thought that by reteaming Jan and John, the star and producer of *White Line Fever*, that they would have another hit, forgetting about the script and me and my work on *White Line Fever*."

Columbia and Jan, by mutual consent, did little to promote *Shadow of the Hawk*, which came and went from theaters in the blink of an eye. *Shadow of the Hawk* marked the end of the relationship between Columbia and Jan, a relationship that had yielded only one moneymaking film, *White Line Fever*, out of the five films of Jan's the studio distributed.

Jan had not turned out to be the next James Dean, Paul Newman, Robert Redford; he had regressed. That experiment ended in 1976 and would never be restarted.

The $1 million payday Jan received for *Damnation Alley*, the post-apocalyptic science fiction film he made for 20th Century Fox, was commensurate with the film's budget, a number that was initially set at $7.5 million when filming began in June 1976, which increased to $17 million throughout the course of the production. The film, and Jan, turned out to be a colossal waste of money and time.

Although the $1 Million milestone was significant for Jan, his film career was severely damaged by the failure of *Damnation Alley*, a film which is best remembered for its fateful proximity to *Star Wars*, the "other" science fiction film Fox bankrolled in 1976, which began filming, in Tunisia, in March 1976. *Star Wars* obviously revolutionized Hollywood and its economic structure following its release in May 1977. *Star Wars* increased Fox's profits by nearly

400 percent from 1976, whereas *Damnation Alley*, which was released in October 1977, lost millions of dollars, which Fox decided to write-off.

The failure of *Damnation Alley* (1977) signaled the end of Jan's film career.

While filming on *Damnation Alley* began in the desert terrain of Borrego Springs, California, in the last week of June, *Star Wars*—which entered production with a budget of $7.5 million, a number that eventually grew to $11 million—was still in production, in London, England. There was serious pessimism toward *Star Wars* at 20th Century Fox, in the mind of the studio's then president, Alan Ladd, Jr., who believed, throughout the summer of 1976, that *Damnation Alley* was going to be the studio's big film of the year—either 1976 or 1977. "Alan Ladd was so excited about *Damnation Alley*, and he told me it was either going to be their big Christmas film of 1976 or their big summer film of 1977," recalls Paul Maslansky, *Damnation Alley*'s producer. "He talked about this other science fiction film that was being shot in England, *Star Wars*, and he said that all he was seeing was this blue screen footage, which was a mess, and that George Lucas had spent lots of money but still didn't have a finished film."

Jan's salary was also reflected in his top billing, above George Peppard, Paul Winfield, and Dominique Sanda, a gorgeous French actress who had, several years earlier, been brought over to Hollywood, which made very poor use of her throughout the decade.

The script for *Damnation Alley*, which was based—loosely, as it turned out, a result of the film's interminable post-production phase—on Roger Zelazny's novel of the same name, elicited an enthusiastic reaction from all parties involved, including Jan, who quickly established a warm rapport with his costars, and with director Jack Smight, who'd only had brief contact with Jan during the *Shadow of the Hawk* fiasco. There were no problems with Jan. "It was Alan Ladd who wanted Jan, who brought great physicality to the role and got along well with everybody—with me, with George Peppard and Jack Smight," says Maslansky. "Jan liked to ride motorbikes, which he did in the film, and he seemed very athletic and strong. I saw no problems with Jan and no signs of alcoholism."

Damnation Alley opens with Jan's character, Lt. Jake Tanner, who ends up presiding over the emergence of World War III from his post at an ICBM silo, which is hidden inside an Air Force missile base in the California desert. Tanner is joined at his post by Major Denton, played by Peppard, and when the United States detects incoming nuclear missiles from the Soviet Union, Denton and Tanner launch a retaliatory strike.

Two years after the strikes, with the Earth tilted off its axis and the planet besieged by massive storms, Denton and Tanner, who have left the base behind, search for other survivors, avoiding mutated insects, traveling, with the remaining others from the base, in two Air Force "Land Masters," giant twelve-wheeled armored personnel carriers, which are capable of climbing difficult inclines and can function in water. The title, *Damnation Alley*, refers to the radiation-filled territory the characters attempt to cross in the film.

Jan with Dominique Sanda in *Damnation Alley*.

Damnation Alley's sizable budget, which isn't visible in the finished film, created more problems than advantages for the production team. It certainly didn't lessen the technical challenges the production faced throughout the filming schedule, which proved fatal. Building the two Land Master vehicles that appear in the film, for example, was an expensive, laborious process. They cost $350,000 each.

Compared to the difficult—futile, as it turned out—task of bringing the story's effects to life, this was money well spent, if only because the Land Masters were the only technical element that worked properly. This was the era of hard effects; there were few optical effects houses around in 1976, and the technical problems that *Damnation Alley* faced, that doomed the film, could not be solved by throwing money at them.

The film, and Jan, needed a time machine—to move their arrival to another point in time, in which their potential could have been more fully realized and understood. If *Damnation Alley*, whose technical credits seemed outdated and shoddy in 1977, had been made a decade later, with the benefit of the maturation of visual effects technology, it might have been Jan's *Star Wars*.

The most difficult effects for the makers of *Damnation Alley* to bring to life were the mutated insects, the cockroaches and scorpions that threaten the characters in the story. Props were used initially, but the footage that appeared in dailies was unconvincing. Then a cockroach wrangler was consulted, and over a thousand hissing cockroaches were imported from Madagascar, the real cockroaches used in conjunction with the fake ones, again with disappointing results. The eventual solution was to photograph real cockroaches and scorpions against the live action footage, using the blue screen process, which was done in post-production, when 20th Century Fox seized control of the film from Smight.

The release, which was originally scheduled for December, near Christmas, ended up being delayed ten months so that optical effects could be superimposed on the sky in almost every shot of the film, to make it appear as if the sky was radioactive, an attempt to better establish, visually, the story's post-apocalyptic atmosphere.

Damnation Alley took in less than $10 million at the box office domestically, following its release in October 1977, and there was no solace to be found overseas, where 20th Century Fox marketed the film, heavily, as a sure-fire blockbuster. "If *Damnation Alley* had been a hit, I think Jan would've had the same kind of career from then on that Harrison Ford had," says Maslansky. "Jan's film career kind of lost momentum at this point, which is a shame."

Harrison Ford, Jan's colleague from *Journey to Shiloh* and the brief period when they were both represented by Dick Clayton, did not become a full-fledged star in the immediate aftermath of the release of *Star Wars*, but *Star Wars*, and the role of Han Solo, gave Ford the platform for stardom that Jan never had.

Star Wars allowed Ford—whose career was floundering just a few years earlier, when Jan was on the rise—a lengthy grace period, which glossed over several post-*Star Wars* failures—*Force Ten from Navarone* (1978), *Hanover Street* (1979), and *The Frisco Kid* (1979), —on the way to his star-making role as Indiana Jones in the film *Raiders of the Lost Ark* (1981).

Damnation Alley turned Jan into a footnote.

5

Wave Goodbye

After completing filming on *Damnation Alley*, in August 1976, Jan went nearly a year without work. Jan—who, by the dawn of 1977, had been a member of the Malibu surfing community for a decade—spent much of this time near the ocean, and on the outskirts of the beach, which was lined with beach houses and shacks that surfers had rented since the 1940s. Jan had his own house, a notorious party house, where he unleashed his darkest impulses.

Jan tried to reconcile with Bonnie in the spring of 1977; Jan, Bonnie, and Amber, who turned three in May 1977, were together when Jan made his return to acting with the film *Big Wednesday* (1978), a coming-of-age story of three surfing friends growing up in the 1960s, which began filming in July 1977.

Big Wednesday—which takes place between 1962 and 1974, when Jan's age ranged between eighteen and thirty—was the last film where Jan, who turned thirty-three in the first week of filming, was able to project the boyishness and vulnerability he had radiated in *Baby Blue Marine*, which was filmed only two years earlier.

His ungodly vitality could no longer disguise the ravages of his lifestyle, which was visible in his face in *Hooper*, Jan's next film, which turned out to be Jan's last major studio film. The reunion with Bonnie did not survive *Big Wednesday* either, and they never got so close to getting back together, as a couple and a happy family, again.

As much as Jan dreamed of getting paid to surf, he does very little actual surfing in the film, where most of his character's surfing scenes are performed by Jan's double, surfing luminary Bill Hamilton, with assistance from surfer Jay Riddle, who was a friend of Jan's and a member of his party group.

Jan is helped by Gary Busey and William Katt in *Big Wednesday* (1978).

Jan's character in the film, Matt Johnson, was based on Lance Carson, a brilliant but self-destructive surfer who did not look much like Jan but was a dead ringer for a young Jeff Bridges, who was a top candidate for the part.

"Jan was handsome, and he looked fit, and he was, it seemed to me, in his prime," says Hamilton. "He was a movie star, and, for a movie star, he was a good surfer, who needed more practice, more time in the water, to be a great surfer. He needed to surf a lot more than he was when we started working on the film."

Big Wednesday's co-writer and director, John Milius, was inspired by his surfing adventures in the 1960s, when Milius was a lifeguard at Zuma Beach, north of Malibu, and then a film student at the University of Southern California, where George Lucas was one of his classmates. In the early 1970s, Milius was one of Hollywood's highest-paid screenwriters, which allowed him to transition to directing features, beginning with the gangster film *Dillinger* (1973), which was followed by the adventure-romance *The Wind and the Lion* (1975), both of which were modest successes, commercially and critically, and encouraged the belief, not unlike what had happened with Jan, that Milius was on the verge of a commercial breakthrough—a blockbuster success similar to those experienced by George Lucas and Steven Spielberg, friends who left him in the dust.

It's easy to see how Warner Bros., the studio that agreed to finance *Big Wednesday*, which began filming with a $7 million budget, might've thought that *Big Wednesday* was going to be another *American Graffiti*. This is what Lucas and Spielberg believed when they agreed to exchange profit points, from Lucas' *Star Wars* and Spielberg's *Close Encounters of the Third Kind* (1977), with Milius and *Big Wednesday*. Everyone has heard that now tired story, but it serves to put the reputations of *Big Wednesday* and Milius, both of which are wildly overstated, in their proper context. *Big Wednesday*'s failure did mortal damage to Jan's film career.

Milius was drawn to lawless, sovereign-free landscapes and found his desolate paradise in the ocean, the last unconquered frontier in the sixties—Milius wasn't interested in science fiction and space. The same revisionism that Milius—who considered the Vietnam War to be a California war, because of how many surfers he had seen go to Vietnam—injected into his post-modern westerns applied to his relationship with surfing, especially in terms of how he viewed himself within the Malibu surfing crowd that kept him at arm's length. "John was never accepted by the surfing community, and I think he made the film to reflect how he wanted things to be," says Hamilton, who was later involved in a bitter litigation process with Milius related to the film. "He was never accepted by the in-crowd and was always outside of that group."

Jan, like Matt Johnson, was Milius' requisite renegade, a sinewy version of Conan the Barbarian transplanted to Malibu, though Milius, who hadn't met Jan prior to their first meeting in Milius' office at Warner Bros., was initially unaware of the similarities between Jan and Matt, which were more clearly observed by Dennis Aaberg, Milius' co-writer and friend, who had met Jan in 1976, near Jan's house in Topanga. "I knew that Jan was from Hanford and had an alcoholic dad," says Aaberg, the younger brother of noted surfer Kemp Aaberg. "Jan was a member of the surfing community and was good friends with surfers Jay Riddle and George Trafton, and Jan was very much into the rowdy, wild Topanga surfing party scene. Everyone had their own party house, and Jan had his, and there were lots of drugs and partying."

Bill Hamilton, who had appeared in several surfing footage-based films, did a screen test at Warner Bros. for the Matt Johnson role but was rejected by *Big Wednesday*'s producer, Buzz Feitshans, who felt that the Matt Johnson role, the film's lead role, required a name actor. Milius' first choice was Jeff Bridges. However, Bridges and Milius could not agree on money. "Jeff Bridges in the film *Stay Hungry* looked exactly like Lance Carson, the inspiration for Matt Johnson," says Aaberg. "Jeff, according to John, wanted too much money. *Big Wednesday* had a budget of $7 million but was originally going to be a little $3 million movie. However, the executive producers [Tamara Asseyev and Alex Rose] did not want there to be the perception that this was a B-movie. Alex and Tamara thought that Jan was a big name star and would be good for the film. I knew Jan and thought he was a great actor; I loved his performance in *Tribes*. I recommended Jan to John, who also liked Jan."

Gary Busey was cast as Leroy Smith, whose nickname is "The Masochist," and William Katt was cast as Jack Barlowe, the most pragmatic, responsible part of the trio. Jan bonded with Busey and Katt immediately; they all drank heavily throughout the filming schedule, often together, while Jan and Busey—Busey followed up *Big Wednesday* by playing the title role in the film *The Buddy Holly Story* (1978), which brought him an Oscar nomination—did cocaine together during breaks in filming, the beginning of a long friendship.

Jan and Busey were on the same trajectory in the late 1970s; what happened to Jan in the mid-1980s was supposed to happen to Busey, who nearly killed himself prior to Jan's degeneration on *Airwolf*, which Busey witnessed firsthand, from inside Jan's trailer on the Universal lot. However, Busey was able to make a successful comeback in the late 1980s, beginning with the film *Lethal Weapon* (1987), a resurgence that lasted for nearly a decade, a comeback that Jan, whose downward spiral was without an end, was neither deserving of nor prepared for.

Although Jan, Busey, and Katt were best-suited to their respective roles, the experiences and traits of the three friends in the film were spread out among the lives of the three actors. Jan and Katt had both done time in the National Guard, both avoiding Vietnam, where Jack is sent in the film.

Jan was the best surfer of the three, followed by Katt, who had surfed quite a bit when he was younger, while Busey had never surfed at all prior to the start of filming. Jan knew the feeling of waking up on the beach after an alcohol-induced blackout, which is how Matt Johnson is introduced to the audience in the film's opening scene.

None of Jan's friendships in Malibu, in or out of the water, approached the intensity of the bond that exists between Matt and his friends in the film. The last time Jan had felt such a connection was in Hanford, with his three surfing buddies, whom he had not seen in several years.

He certainly did not have an elder in his life, either in Hollywood or at the beach, like Bear, played in the film by Sam Melville. Bear is a thirty-something surfing historian (modeled after Milius), who runs a surfboard shaping business on the Malibu pier. Bear is a guru and mentor to Matt and his friends, and he is a keeper of Milius' own philosophizing about surfing, which Jan, correctly, felt Milius had injected too much of into the script, which had grown to 144 pages by the start of filming. Jan didn't think this would work and shared this with Milius, whom Jan found to be genial, talented but stubborn to the idea of dialogue and story changes.

For his double in the surfing scenes, Jan originally wanted to be paired with world champion surfer Peter Townend, a friend of Jan's, who looked nothing like Jan but bore a more than passable resemblance to Katt, which led to their pairing, while Australian surfer Ian Cairns was hired to handle Busey's water scenes.

Besides the immeasurable difference in skill, Jan and Matt Johnson—Hamilton's Matt Johnson—had very different styles when they were on their surfboards. Hamilton is a stylist, which is visible in the way Matt tiptoes, walks across the board, the opposite of Jan, who was very upright on his board, always keeping his head up, facing the shore, the result of Jan needing to wear contact lenses.

Most of the surfing scenes were filmed in civil war-wracked El Salvador, where the water was full of baby sharks, and was polluted, which led to most of the cast and crew being stricken with amoebic dysentery but not Jan, who developed a nagging ear infection.

Additional beach and water scenes were filmed at the Hollister Ranch in Santa Barbara, and at Sunset Beach in Hawaii, which was the setting for the finale, where the three friends, in 1974, get back together, presumably for the last time, to surf the Great Swell, a rare ocean event—consisting of thunderous waves and towering faces that produce enough water to flood a small town—that happens once every twenty years. "The happiest I saw Jan during the filming was when I was standing on a rock and watching Jan in the water, surfing, standing on the nose of the board," says Hamilton. "I watched Jan try to make the wave, and when he did make the wave, he looked at me and pumped his fist in the air. It was a real moment of triumph for him."

The production spent five weeks in El Salvador and seven weeks at Sunset Beach, and Amber (who plays Matt's daughter, Melissa, in parts of the film) and Bonnie spent a week with Jan in El Salvador. "Jan had Amber and Bonnie with him in El Salvador, and it looked to me like he loved his family very much," says Hamilton. "Jan was very private, though; he would leave the location, and his family, and go off somewhere and then return to the location when needed."

One night, in El Salvador, Jan was in a bar, where he got into a drinking contest with Terry Leonard, *Big Wednesday*'s stunt coordinator. "Terry, himself, was a heavy drinker, and Jan and Terry had a drinking contest one night, downing big shots of tequila," says Aaberg. "Then Jan started taking massive chugs, as if he couldn't get enough of it into him, and I was amazed by how much he could chug down at one time. It didn't seem to affect him. It was scary to watch."

The arc of Jan's character throughout the film, between 1962 and 1974, mirrored Jan's life up until 1977. Matt's drunkenness consumes the first half of the film, which separates him from Jack, who, in 1965, is inducted, voluntarily, into the army and sent to Vietnam, where he spends three years. By the time Jack returns, in 1968, Matt, though still reckless, has embraced the roles of father and husband, which Jan was set to let go of by the end of filming.

The most telling scene in the film, for Jan, happens in 1965, after a drunken Matt is thrown off the beach by Jack, who is a lifeguard. Matt—who is looked up to as a hero by the kids on the beach, which sickens him—goes to see Bear at the thriving surf shop Bear has opened after his former beach pier location was condemned. After a depressed Matt enters Bear's shop, which has been sponsoring Matt in the local surfing contests, Matt tells Bear, his surrogate father, that he does not want to surf anymore—that he does not want to be famous and does not want kids to look up to a worthless drunk like himself. "Jan did not like himself very much and felt that he didn't deserve his success," says Aaberg. "I thought, as an actor, that he was a natural, and I loved what he did with the character, especially during the scene in the draft depot, where Jan's character wears a leg brace to get out of being sent to Vietnam, which was just what my little brother did."

Big Wednesday's esoteric nature was embedded in the film's title, a reference to an epic day in Malibu, when the waves are utterly transcendent. The arcane title was almost certainly fatal to the film's commercial prospects, even more so than Milius' reliance on bombastic, caricature-based storytelling.

The John Milius Story was never considered, though it would not have seemed less ambiguous than *Big Wednesday* appeared to the teen and young adult audience Warner Bros. was hoping to court, to whom it sounded like a maudlin drama, clearly intended for their stodgy parents. Was this a sequel to *Ash Wednesday*, the 1973 Elizabeth Taylor flop? Anything else—any title that included the words *Summer* and/or *Surf*—would have been an improvement.

Warner Bros. thought that *Big Wednesday* was going to be a blockbuster in the summer of 1978, which is why the studio released the film at the end of May, hoping that the film would draft off of *Grease* (1978)—which became the biggest hit of the summer—and *Jaws 2* (1978), both of which were released in June. *National Lampoon's Animal House* (1978)—which ended up as the third highest-grossing film of 1978, behind *Grease* and *Superman* (1978)—was released at the end of July, alongside *Hooper*, the Burt Reynolds action-comedy Jan filmed in early 1978, which turned out to be Warner Bros.' only hit of the summer.

Big Wednesday's grosses did not even approach those of Busey's *The Buddy Holly Story*, which was also released in May and was considered a sleeper hit of the summer, largely because of its low production cost. This was a caveat that had no bearing on *Big Wednesday*, whose final cost, including marketing and publicity, ended up being close to $12 million, a total that was much less than that of *Damnation Alley* but even more worrisome for Jan, who had not been responsible for a commercial success since *White Line Fever*, a shining moment that felt, for Jan and his shrinking group of supporters, as if it had happened a lifetime ago—in Hanford maybe.

The dreadful reviews—all of which lambasted the film's downbeat, ham-handed, relentlessly metaphorical presentation—created the first negative impact for everyone involved and laid the foundation for the crippling box office returns (*Big Wednesday* took in under $5 million domestically) that pushed *Big Wednesday* out of theaters within a month.

Jan took the film's disappointing performance personally, and he found no relief in *Hooper*'s success, which bypassed him completely. "It [*Big Wednesday*'s failure] was a crushing blow to everyone, especially Jan," says Aaberg, whose screenwriting career ended with *Big Wednesday*. "After the film's failure, Jan and I took a trip to Scorpion Bay in Mexico. We surfed, and Jan had fun, and everyone who saw him wanted to approach him, especially girls, which made him feel good about himself."

Beyond *Big Wednesday*'s failure and the increasingly fragile state of his career, Jan was most hurt by the negative reaction he received from his surfing friends in Malibu, who were very critical of the film, and of Jan for making a film that exposed their community to the outside world, believing that Jan was one of them, when in fact he belonged nowhere and to no one.

6
The Fall Guy

After the end of filming on *Big Wednesday*, Jan found new representation, enlisting Jim Wiatt of the powerhouse talent agency International Creative Management (better known as ICM) to restore momentum to his lagging career. "Jan was considered hot at the agency," recalls producer Larry Lyttle, who was a literary agent at ICM in the late 1970s. "There was a lot of buzz about Jan, and there was a belief that he was still going to be a major star."

Hooper, which marked the end of Jan's connection to any major Hollywood studio, in this case Warner Bros., was the first film project that was born out of Jan's relationship with ICM. *Hooper* was developed—by its director, former stuntman Hal Needham, and its star, Burt Reynolds—as an homage to stuntmen, Hollywood's most undervalued resource, a group whom Jan had increasingly learned to depend on throughout the 1970s, first for his safety, and then for drugs. At the end of January 1978, Jan's supplier, whom Jan had first met in Tucson, Arizona, during the filming of *White Line Fever*, accompanied Jan to Tuscaloosa, Alabama, for the filming of *Hooper*, which began shooting in the first week of February 1978.

Hooper was the last film that placed Jan inside the apprentice-teacher dynamic, which is a literal interpretation of the relationship that exists in the film, between Reynolds' aging stuntman, Sonny Hooper, who is being forced into retirement because of mounting injuries, and Jan's bold, younger stuntman, who can jump higher, run faster and seems poised not only to inherit the torch from the older Hooper—whom Jan's character, Delmore "Ski" Shidski, professes to worship—but to take it by force if he has to, which turns out to be completely unnecessary.

Reynolds was the most accessible of the superstars Jan worked with in the 1970s—accessibility, and Reynolds' willingness to let the public in on all of his secrets, was the main factor in both Reynolds' rise to superstardom in the late 1970s and his steep decline in the mid-1980s.

Reynolds' popularity was grounded in Southern-based action-comedy films like *Hooper, The Longest Yard* (1974), and his blockbuster, *Smokey and the Bandit* (1977), which grossed more than $100 million domestically and paired him with Sally Field, who joined Reynolds on *Hooper*, where their developing real-life love affair—and the public's endless fascination with their coupling—overwhelmed everyone and everything else that appeared onscreen.

The impact of the Field-Reynolds relationship was not something that Jan and his new representation had reckoned with on *Hooper*, a film in which Jan received second billing—between Reynolds and Field—but ended up as a glorified extra. The sheer attractiveness of a surefire hit was reassuring enough to Jan to make him perfectly willing to play the role of second banana opposite Reynolds, as he had against Bronson. It was the shock of being a third wheel that threw him off balance.

This dynamic took shape very early during the filming in Tuscaloosa, where the unspoiled locals immediately clamored for a sighting of America's newly-minted It couple, who were very obliging with the crowds, while Jan stood behind them, smiling and waving, his presence unnecessary here and throughout the film.

Reynolds was, at his height, a twenty-four karat movie star, a latter-day Clark Gable, a model of self-deprecating humor and a virile breed. Jan, who was given less than a hundred words to say in the film, was no match for this wall of charm and masculinity, which manifested itself as a personality cult populated by a loyal group of sycophants—they were Reynolds' cronies and yes-men—which functioned very much like Elvis Presley's Memphis Mafia.

For Jan to come off effectively against this hyper level of energy and magnetism, he had to appear as a threat to Reynolds' character, and to Reynolds himself, who was only vaguely aware—and barely concerned—about the approach of Arnold Schwarzenegger and Sylvester Stallone, the latter representing the most immediate threat to Reynolds' standing as America's number one box office draw, a title that Reynolds held between 1978 and 1982. This was a mission that Jan was never ready for.

Jan is competent and smooth in the film but poses no threat to Reynolds, who is less than ten years older than Jan but appears in the film as Jan's father figure, or a sardonic uncle, not a brother, a colleague. This is yet another morose example of Jan's identity crisis, which did not at all lessen for Jan in his thirties. The normalization of Jan's aging process, which was restored in the early eighties, was only achieved through alcohol and cocaine.

By the end of the 1970s, there was no one else in Jan's space—the space of an actor who was approaching his mid-thirties but was still The Kid, which is how Reynolds' character addresses Jan in the film. Jan, at the age of thirty-three, still did not fit neatly into any single generation; he had less in common with Reynolds and anyone else within ten years of him than he did with the approaching generation of young actors—Nicolas Cage, Tom Cruise, Timothy Hutton, Sean Penn, all of whom are at least fifteen years younger than Jan, all of whom were unknown to him, and the world, at this point, except for Penn, who babysat Amber several times.

Jan could not keep up with Burt Reynolds in *Hooper* (1978).

With Ski, Jan had never been given a role so lacking in personal resonance, so inconsequential to the film's success, which is true even in the film's thrilling stunt sequences, in which Jan's presence was only required for establishing shots. He is an automaton in the film, whose only purpose is to tickle Reynolds, who—more than any other star of his generation—did not need any assistance in this department.

This is why the success of *Hooper* did not move Jan's film career from its standstill position. *Hooper* grossed nearly $80 million domestically—it was Reynolds' biggest box office success after *Smokey and the Bandit*. *Hooper*—along with *The End* (1978), the third film Field and Reynolds appeared in together, with Reynolds directing—cemented the goldenness of the Field-

Reynolds pairing, which ended, both personally and professionally, during the filming of *Smokey and the Bandit II* (1980). Jan was barely mentioned in *Hooper*'s press materials.

In terms of Jan's career, the success of *Hooper* was secondary in the minds of Hollywood studio executives to the failures of *Big Wednesday* and *Damnation Alley*, both of which Jan had been held responsible for. Jan was viewed as a tangential element of *Hooper*, not because of his screen time—which was considerable, more than that of Field—but because of the timidity he displays the film, which was interpreted, even by many of the same people who had predicted stardom for Jan a few years earlier, as an unwillingness on Jan's part to fight for his career.

By the late 1970s, Jan's process of regeneration was no longer the result of genetics but rather surfing, which became a form of detoxification for Jan, years before he began entering professional chemical dependency programs and rehab facilities, one after the other, none of which produced such impressive results.

Before he'd started work on *Hooper*, Jan—with the help of friend and champion surfer Gerry Lopez, who appears in *Big Wednesday*—went to Hawaii for two weeks to get cleaned up, rarely drinking, avoiding drugs, getting himself in the best physical condition he could, anticipating the inevitable slide that would take place during filming.

The extended pauses between films were becoming more and more dangerous for Jan, and, following the end of filming on Hooper, six months went by before Jan directed his mind back toward his career, or had to, given the paucity of film offers that Jan and his agent, Jim Wiatt, received in the spring of 1978, most of which now—for the first time in nearly a decade—were from independent companies. The film offers were now mingled with a chorus of television producers, who called to inquire as to whether Jan would consider moving back to television, a format Jan had avoided since 1975, following his second appearance on *Police Story*.

In August 1978, in the wake of *Hooper*'s successful release, Wiatt attempted to package Jan into *Hard Country*, a film project based on the urban cowboy lifestyle, inspired by a Country & Western song that was written by singer-songwriter Michael Martin Murphey, who was also an ICM client. Wiatt recruited screenwriter Michael Kane to go to Texas with Murphey to flesh out the characters and story, and then Wiatt approached Warner Bros., who agreed to put the project on the fast track, with Jan attached as star.

This fell apart in September, either on or shortly after September 12, 1978, when *Esquire* magazine published "The Ballad of the Urban Cowboy: America's Search for True Grit," an article by writer Aaron Latham, which became the basis for Paramount Pictures' film *Urban Cowboy*, starring John Travolta, which was released in June 1980.

Scrambling but wanting to forestall a move back to television—where so many of Jan's films found their largest audience—Jan and Wiatt pondered the available film offers and settled on the action-drama *Defiance* (1980), which was eventually distributed by American International Pictures, a highly-active independent—mostly in exploitation and horror—that became defunct in 1980, following a string of box office flops, including *Defiance*.

Defiance was the first independent film project for Jan since he entered *The Bandits*, and *Defiance*'s elements, the production's main ingredients, were impeccable. *Defiance* was one of the first titles in the career of producer Jerry Bruckheimer, *Defiance* preceding *Flashdance* (1983), *Beverly Hills Cop* (1984), and *Top Gun* (1986)—all blockbuster hits for the future mega-producer, whose biography contains no mention of *Defiance*, which represented Jan's last bid to prove that he was a bankable commodity in film, before he had to seriously contemplate a return to television. "I had not worked in a long time, and this was the best script that came along" —this was how Jan explained his involvement.

Defiance was directed by John Flynn, a gritty action specialist, who had done particularly good work in his most recent film, the violent revenge thriller *Rolling Thunder* (1977). Before the start of filming in New York, which began in the last week of October, Jan, as he had done before he started filming *Hooper*, went surfing in Hawaii for two weeks, with Lopez, whom Jan was reluctant to drink around. The results were spectacular; Jan looked more athletic, present, and strong in *Defiance* than he had since the filming of *Baby Blue Marine*, and he never looked so good again. "Jan drank very heavily during the filming," recalled Flynn, who died in 2007. "He'd be drinking in the morning—he'd be sitting with a bottle of Heineken, which was his breakfast. It quickly became obvious, to me and the rest of the cast and crew, that Jan lacked confidence and didn't believe in himself. He was embarrassed to be an actor; he was always worried that people were staring at him and laughing at him behind his back, and so I would have to constantly reassure him that he was doing a good job, which he did, for the most part, when he wasn't so drunk that we had to prop him up for filming."

Flynn was a director who reveled in authenticity, especially in his choice of filming locations, and he did not have to look far for inspiration in New York City, which resembled a bloody futuristic wasteland at the time. *Defiance*'s story takes place in the Lower East Side, which was gang-infested, and Flynn insisted on bringing the cast and crew there for the start of filming, ignoring the presence of the gangs, who dominated Lower Manhattan and menaced the production during the New York filming, which lasted two weeks. The production then moved to Los Angeles, where the film was completed, where the production encountered the grisly work of Bobby Joe Maxwell, better known as the Skid Row Stabber, an occultist and ritual slayer of homeless men, who had yet to be apprehended.

Until Flynn reached an accord with the gangs, they hurled .22 caliber pellets at the film trucks with slingshots, exploding windshields. Flynn ended up alleviating the threat by hiring members of a local karate club—most of whom were gang members themselves—to provide security and serve as location scouts. The transient nature of this agreement was highlighted, during the filming, when a woman was murdered in the area, shot to death. A machete-wielding man was also arrested.

Flynn approached Jan with the same expectation of negotiation; he had heard bad things about Jan before they met, which may have defeated this relationship before Jan arrived in New York, where Jan—who had never been exposed to gangs outside of his trips to Los Angeles—quickly grasped the rules of this landscape and these violent tribes, whose order he found similar to his band of surfers. Jan, as Flynn had, looked for the leader of the local gang, and, like Flynn, recognized the need to pay him off, in order to ensure his safety and that of the rest of the cast and crew. However, there were many gangs in the area, and they all had leaders who insisted on being paid.

In the film, Jan plays Tommy Gamble, a merchant seaman, who, as the film opens, has been suspended for six months. Stuck in New York, Tommy takes up residence in a rundown apartment building on the gang-ridden Lower East Side. While he waits for his next assignment, Tommy befriends his neighbors, who are being terrorized by a murderous street gang called the Souls. Tommy ends up fighting the Souls, while he tries to convince the intimidated locals to stand up for themselves.

The most identifiable aspect of Tommy Gamble, in terms of Jan's own life, is Tommy's artistry, which he displays through his watercolor paintings. Jan, who many believe would've been a sign painter at this point in his life, had he not become an actor, had scarcely painted since his time at Ventura College, an era of his life—prior to his fateful first meeting with Dick Clayton—that Jan had become increasingly nostalgic for, wondering—as many of his Hanford colleagues have debated—where this parallel universe would've placed him at this point in his life.

Besides the opening shot of the film, which takes place on a dock, the New York setting was completely alien to Jan, who had barely spent any time on the East Coast. Other than the presence of the gangs, Jan found a supportive environment, particularly within the film's stellar cast, which includes Danny Aiello, Oscar winner Art Carney, Rudy Ramos, and Theresa Saldana. "The first time I met Jan was on a rooftop in New York City," says Ramos, who plays Angel, the leader of the Souls, Tommy's nemesis in the film. "I had tried to stay away from him, because he was the good guy in the film, and I was the bad guy. I wandered away from everyone during a break and ran into him when he was standing on one end of the rooftop, just looking at a view of New York City from there. I started to turn away, when he turned and saw me and said hello. I said hello, and then, after a long pause, we both sat on the ledge and started talking. We hit it off right away and found that we had much in common other than acting. We were both from small towns, and neither of us had come to Los Angeles to pursue acting. He was such a good guy and so humble. I had heard so many negative things about him, and I didn't see it at all."

According to Flynn, Jan developed a close bond with costar Aiello during the filming in New York, to the point where Jan started giving some of his own dialogue to Aiello in their scenes. "Jan loved Danny and latched onto him during the filming and tried to give some of his lines to Danny," said Flynn. "I told Jan, who was very sweet and didn't have any kind of movie star ego, that he couldn't do this."

Ramos, who had a twenty-year friendship with Jan, disagrees with this description of Jan's behavior and recalls Jan as being very engaged during the filming, making creative suggestions to Flynn, who gave Jan's ideas little weight. "He was not drinking heavily during the filming of *Defiance*," says Ramos. "He was easy to work with and, with his great stunt skills, really protected me during our great fight scene. Everybody loved Danny, Theresa, Mr. Carney, and Jan, who was very well liked by the cast and crew. John Flynn was a wonderful director and a nice guy, but he wouldn't listen to suggestions from Jan. I heard some of Jan's ideas, and I thought they would work, and I felt bad for Jan when that would happen in front of the cast and crew."

Defiance received a limited theatrical release in March 1980—it was the least publicized film of Jan's since *Shadow of the Hawk* and was completely ignored by audiences and dismissed by critics as a comic book fantasy and a knockoff of *Death Wish*. *Defiance*'s obscurity, which has passed over time, was, on some level, a much worse fate than the loud disappointments that were *Big Wednesday* and *Damnation Alley*. Jan was not, as he had believed, happy on the fringe; he was not happy anywhere.

Although *Defiance* served to lessen the growing doubts in Hollywood about Jan's physical condition, it failed to construct an action movie persona around Jan, which is what Jan and his representation were hoping the film would accomplish when Jan signed on. Jan was not an action star; he lacked a martial arts background, a shadowy history, and did not look or feel comfortable with a gun in his hand.

Jan thought of himself as a journeyman.

7
Endangered Species

The making of *Defiance* was followed by a full year of inactivity in Jan's career, heralding the next phase of Jan's career and life, the beginning of his continuing final chapter, where everything that happened off screen overshadowed anything that happened on it.

Item: September 13, 1979. Jan's endless legal troubles begin, when sheriff's deputies discover a greenhouse full of marijuana plants on Jan's Encinal Canyon property in Malibu. The marijuana activity was first noticed by a police helicopter lurking overhead, and when deputies raided the property, following the issuance of a search warrant, they counted forty-one plants, whose height ranged between four and twelve feet, weighing 150 pounds. He was charged with the cultivation of marijuana, which was later dismissed, and marijuana possession, which he pleaded guilty to during a February 1980 hearing, where he was fined $500 and given a year of probation.

This first arrest, the first of many, received infinitely more coverage than Jan's next film, *Hard Country*, a project that Jim Wiatt resuscitated after it had collapsed the previous year at Warner Bros. Warner Bros. let the film go after finding out about Paramount's intention to go forward with their own honky-tonk themed film project, *Urban Cowboy*, whose filming was completed in November 1979, one month before *Hard Country*—which had a budget of $6 million—began filming in Bakersfield, California, a filming location that was chosen to double for Martin County, Texas, where the film is set.

Jan, a country blues aficionado, knew the Bakersfield scene, which inspired him—along with the encouragement of musician friends Roger Miller, Willie Nelson, Leon Russell, James Taylor—to write songs, several of which he cut tracks for. None of the songs were released, beyond his circle, and should not be.

He sang much better following the 1996 car crash that broke his neck and damaged his throat to the point where his voice was reduced to a whisper, only because he sounded so soulful and vulnerable, with a croaky twang, which was more authentically broken and tattered than the voice of anyone he knew, even Willie.

Jan's dream of becoming a country music star, though forever unrealized, at least showed that Jan was capable of holding ambitions, which is more than can be said of his character in *Hard Country*, Kyle Richardson, whose immediate goals, like the film's, are spectacularly minor. Kyle only wants to be with his girlfriend, Jodie, played by Kim Basinger in her first film role. She works as a telephone operator, and while she loves Kyle, she sees no future in this rural abyss, which she plans to escape from by taking a job as a flight attendant in Los Angeles.

Hard Country, which was directed by David Greene, is a portrait of a contemporary cowboy who finds himself adrift in the modern world, a characterization aided immeasurably by Jan's increasingly introverted manner and weathered appearance, which deglamorizes Jan as much as the bushy moustache and longish hair he brought to the filming. None of this could hide Jan's surfer's musculature, which is visible throughout the film, incongruous with Jan's beer-guzzling character, the last piece of Jan's beauty to die. This is the best of Jan's later film performances.

Hard Country's modest purpose and its unvarnished visuals of distressed rural life, though refreshing and in support of what is a fairly compelling character study, clearly spoke to a narrow—and narrowing—potential audience, which is not what Jim Wiatt, Jan's agent, at all envisioned when he packaged the film.

Greene was from television, and his cruel typecasting as a television director—his television credits included the acclaimed made-for television film *Friendly Fire* (1979) and the landmark miniseries' *Rich Man, Poor Man* (1976) and *Roots* (1977)—undermined his chances for a feature directing career, which had seemed promising after his acclaimed feature film adaptation of the popular stage musical *Godspell* (1973). The disaster film *Gray Lady Down* (1978), Greene's most recent feature credit, failed miserably at the box office, and Greene was never given another chance after *Hard Country*.

Jan's career could no longer survive the pure, undiluted dose of obscurity that *Hard Country* represented, which Jan himself was inextricably drawn to. On a commercial level, *Hard Country* was a miscalculation from beginning to end; although *Hard Country* and Paramount's glossy *Urban Cowboy* were considered, early on, to be direct competitors, the difference between the two projects is profound, highlighted by the films' musical styles—*Hard Country*'s doleful, dreary wailings versus *Urban Cowboy*'s hit-laden soundtrack, which earned more than $20 million following the film's release and is now credited with launching the country-pop boom in the eighties and nineties.

Another obvious comparison is between Jan and John Travolta, who were completely dissimilar, both in appearance—Jan's basic sullenness and Travolta's perpetual liveliness—and in the state of their careers. Travolta, upon *Urban Cowboy*'s release, was still riding the crest of *Grease* and *Saturday Night Fever* (1977), his two blockbuster successes, and while *Urban Cowboy*, which grossed just under $50 million domestically, was regarded only as a modest success, insignificant compared to *Grease* and *Saturday Night Fever*, it did nothing to hurt Travolta's standing as a box office favorite, a status that was withdrawn in the mid-1980s, when Jan was out of features completely.

Hard Country—which was financed by Marble Arch Productions, the American film production arm of Lord Grade's crumbling entertainment empire—was Jan's second independent film in a row, though the film's distribution was, ultimately, taken over by Universal Pictures, who did little with it. Originally scheduled for a May 1980 release, one month prior to *Urban Cowboy*'s release, *Hard Country* was held back until May 1981. *Hard Country* earned less than $1 Million at the box office.

In 1982, *Hard Country* found a much wider audience on television, when NBC showed the film in primetime, where it generated strong ratings, attracting millions of viewers. Also in 1982, CBS broadcast *Defiance*, which was another ratings success.

Jan was a movie star on television.

8
Reboot

In September 1980, Jan filmed *The Return* (1980), which was the last film Jan made before he was cast in the miniseries *The Winds of War* (1983). *The Return*, which was intended for theatrical release but was ultimately shuttled to cable television in December, marked a turning point in Jan's career, not only in terms of his return to television but also because it was the first time Jan appeared, without any creative justification, so openly drunk on camera.

Jan's disheveled appearance is not so out of place in the film, the most impoverished production Jan was involved with since *The Bandits*, nearly fifteen years earlier. "I contacted Jan's agent to check his availability and price," recalls Greydon Clark, *The Return*'s director and producer. "He accepted the script and got back to me in a few days with Jan's agreement. His price was $250,000 for three weeks. I agreed."

The Return is a science fiction thriller, Jan's first genre film since the ill-fated *Damnation Alley*, a film whose ambition and certainly its prodigious cost—if not its almost equally inept special effects—dwarfed *The Return*, which entered production with a budget of under a million dollars. "A screening of Jan's previous picture, *Defiance*, was arranged," says Clark. "I met Jan at the screening; he was cordial and seemed enthusiastic about doing *The Return*. After Jan left the screening room, I asked his agent about rumors of Jan's drug use. His agent assured me that the rumors were untrue."

Although Jan headlined *The Return*, he wasn't the only performer in the film looking to reignite a stalled career; Jan is joined in the film by Cybill Shepherd, who plays his love interest, as well as Raymond Burr and Martin Landau. All of them would revive their careers, to varying degrees, in the 1980s—Jan's short-lived resurgence began with *The Winds of War*; Cybill Shepherd's comeback was launched with the television series *Moonlighting*, which allowed her, briefly, to reconnect with a film career that had been cold since the mid-1970s; Burr appeared in a string of *Perry Mason* made-for-television films; Landau, whose gaunt appearance increasingly typecast him in freakishly sinister roles in the early 1980s, found new life as a character actor in prestigious films, beginning with his Oscar-nominated supporting performance in *Tucker: The Man and His Dream* (1988).

This was a dispirited bunch that arrived in Piru, California, the small historic town, located in eastern Ventura County, California, where most of the filming took place. The fragile psyches of Jan's costars mirrored Jan's alcoholic ravages, which was not a new phenomenon to Clark, a low budget merchant, who was used to playing the role of amateur psychologist with the faded stars who fell into his lap and was expert at guiding them down into the void that Clark presided over.

Although Jan—whose slurred speech and wobbly gait forced alterations to the compact filming schedule—presented a unique challenge to Clark, who was not above begging Jan to show up sober each day, Clark was otherwise largely unfazed, having decided, correctly, that Jan's involvement outweighed the trouble he created, the calculation that everyone who worked with Jan throughout the 1980s had to make.

Jan's most convincing performances, during this period, took place off screen, when he convinced two of television's foremost authority figures that he had cleaned himself up, beginning with Dan Curtis, the architect of the miniseries *The Winds of War*, followed by Donald P. Bellisario, the creator of *Airwolf*.

The only graceful aspect of Jan's return to television was that he was far from the first actor to make this transition; he looked to James Garner, and to Rock Hudson, his costar in *The Undefeated*, as role models in this process, though the clearest comparable to Jan, at the dawn of 1980, was probably William Devane, an actor, five years older than Jan, whose dogged but failed pursuit of film stardom in the mid to late 1970s made him, by default, an established commodity in the eyes of network executives and television producers.

Devane's transition began with the miniseries *From Here to Eternity* (1979), a lavish adaptation of the 1953 film, which brought Devane the highest salary—he was paid over $1.5 million for his work in the miniseries—that any actor had received for a made-for television production. A short-lived series spinoff followed in 1980, which paid Devane $75,000 per episode. In 1984, Devane joined the cast of the television series *Knots Landing*, a nighttime soap opera, where he remained for several years.

Devane proved that a leading man in film, even one that fell short of stardom, had inflated value on television, a format that was completely segregated from film in the seventies and eighties, a slum. Jan had already proved his value on television, through the ratings that his films had generated, and it was this logic that appealed to Curtis, who was well aware of Jan's expanding reputation for drunkenness but had never seen it in Jan's work—when

Curtis first met Jan, in November 1980, Curtis, like most of Hollywood and the public, had not seen *The Return*.

Still, Curtis, who devoted over a decade of his career and life to bringing Herman Wouk's 1971 novel—and then Wouk's 1978 follow-up novel, *War and Remembrance*—to the small screen, was far from willing to simply hand Jan the part, which he proved by putting Jan (who claimed to have read Wouk's gargantuan 885 page tome before the start of filming, which, if true, would've been the first book of substance that Jan had read in over a decade) through several arduous screen tests.

Jan passed with flying colors; Jan also removed, in Curtis' mind, the burned-in image of Jan as a good old boy who only liked to drive trucks (Curtis was obviously familiar with *White Line Fever*). In doing this, during his readings for Curtis, Jan recovered the keen instincts that had seemingly gone into rebellion in recent years.

Getting the part of Byron Henry—who is the middle child of Robert Mitchum's Navy Commander Victor "Pug" Henry (the miniseries' main protagonist and the conduit through which the viewer is introduced to Franklin Roosevelt, as well as Churchill, Hitler, Mussolini, and Stalin)—meant a year-long commitment for Jan, who had become well-conditioned by this point to working in three to six week intervals—the typical time range of his film shoots—and expending the requisite energy but no more.

It is the all-consuming, nearly twenty-four hour a day responsibility of carrying a television production that many of Jan's supporters point to as one of the main reasons for his collapse on *Airwolf*. Jan was able to negotiate his commitment to *The Winds of War* by rationalizing that the project—whose script surpassed 1,000 pages in length, relative to the miniseries' 883 minute running time, which was spread over seven nights in February 1983—was the equivalent of seven or eight feature films, divided into the miniseries' $40 million budget.

It also helped that Jan—who received third billing, behind Mitchum and Ali MacGraw—did not have to do the heavy lifting, which fell to Mitchum, Jan's costar from *Going Home*, who was, in his early sixties, still much more able in this regard than was Jan. With Mitchum standing over him, Jan was able to melt into the background while still occupying a leading role. He felt much more comfortable here, in a supporting position, where his brief, concentrated bursts of energy had maximum impact. He benefitted more from the miniseries than anyone else in the cast.

Despite *The Winds of War*'s lofty pretensions, Jan, who was paid $50,000 per week, was, indisputably, part of a second team cast, which was the clearest symbol of the stark separation between film and television—and the scarcity of crossover—that existed in this era.

Besides Mitchum and MacGraw, the over forty group in the cast was filled by the likes of Polly Bergen, Peter Graves, John Houseman. Jan was joined in the younger category by David Dukes, Lisa Eilbacher, and Ben Murphy—they were three promising young faces in the early eighties, all now long forgotten.

The Winds of War—which covers events from March 1939 until America's entry into World War II in December 1941, following Japan's attack on Pearl Harbor—was filmed all over the world: England, Germany, Italy, the United States, and Zagreb in the former Yugoslavia, which was the most barren of the locations, where the only source of entertainment was a government-run disco and an odd assortment of Russian-made *Pac-Man* machines. It was here where Jan did most of his drinking during the fourteen-month production schedule, joined regularly by Mitchum, with whom Jan quickly rekindled the warm camaraderie that had passed between them during the filming of *Going Home*.

There were several scattered breaks for the cast and crew throughout 1981; Jan returned to Malibu in the summer of 1981 and went sailing on a $250,000 boat he purchased. Money was not a concern.

The subject of Jan's alcoholism has become so repetitive at this point that it no longer warrants mention, except where it directly affects his career and health. Cocaine had become nearly as repetitive of a subject by this point; *The Winds of War* now seems like a loving snapshot of the prelude to the heroin, smack, and the needles.

His various chemical and psychological issues accumulated and destroyed him on *Airwolf* but were closeted during the filming of *The Winds of War*, where the problems that Jan's behavior caused for the production were manageable and outweighed by the unexpected qualities that *The Winds of War* brought out in Jan, which he was never able to tap into again. However, Jan was not brought back for *War and Remembrance*.

Chief among Jan's few remaining virtues was a keen sense of honor, which he channeled through his thoughts of his father, former World War II bomber pilot Lloyd, who was very enthusiastic about the miniseries and barely aware of Jan's problems. Jan was usually groggy but sober whenever he spoke to his parents, and when he was with Amber, who was nine when the miniseries aired and a straight A student in school, in Sun Valley, Idaho, where she was an avid horseback rider and skier. Jan was very proud of her.

The most common thread between Byron Henry—a Columbia University graduate who holds a naval reserve commission—and dropout Jan is their uncommitted states at the time of filming. Byron is uncommitted toward a possible career, and Jan felt the same way about acting by the end of 1980, less than twenty years after leaving Hanford to attend Ventura College.

Byron, in 1939, takes a job as a research assistant for Aaron Jastrow, a Jewish author, which is how he ends up meeting Jastrow's niece, Natalie, played by MacGraw, whom Byron falls in love with and eventually marries. Natalie is three years older than Byron, while MacGraw is six years older than Jan, who was thirty-six when filming began. The age difference appears to be much greater than this, and MacGraw, who was attempting her own comeback at the time, was savaged by the critics, as much for her motherly appearance as her performance in the miniseries, while Jan, who was credited for filling the heroic core of the miniseries, received his best personal notices since *Buster and Billie*, from the television critics, many of whom proclaimed Jan as the breakout star from the miniseries, ignoring, or forgetting, his decade-long film career.

Jan—who spent three months sailing in the Caribbean after the end of filming on *The Winds of War*—only made one feature film between the spring of 1980 and the end of 1986. This was *Last Plane Out* (1983), which was another independent production; it is a political thriller, in which Jan plays an American journalist who falls in love with a Sandinista rebel while covering the civil war in Nicaragua, a subject that Jan had become familiar with while filming *Big Wednesday* in El Salvador.

Like *Defiance* and *Hard Country*, *Last Plane Out*—which began filming in Miami in June 1982—received a token theatrical release. It was released on less than a hundred screens in September 1983, and then it was tossed into the now thriving video market that Jan later lived in, beginning in the late 1980s.

Between February 6 and February 13 of 1983, the period in which ABC broadcast *The Winds of War*'s seven installments, Jan was exposed to eighty million sets of eyeballs— this was the average number of viewers that the miniseries garnered during this period, which was measured by an average nightly rating of 38.6 and a 54 share, a whopping performance—unfathomable in today's increasingly cable and niche-driven television universe—that surpassed the miniseries *Shogun* (1980), second only to *Roots*.

Jan—who was sent on a promotional tour by ABC, which he fully participated in— received his second Golden Globe nomination for the miniseries, in the supporting category, losing to Richard Kiley, who won for his performance in the miniseries *The Thorn Birds*.

The Winds of War, which was also very successful overseas, made Jan internationally famous, which is not the same as being an international star, though Jan had already won a sizable European following because of *The World's Greatest Athlete*.

He acted like someone who needed to hide from the world for his own protection in the spring of 1983, in the aftermath of the miniseries' airing, when Jan hid in his oceanfront house, and on the water, with no professional commitments, except for the verbal agreement he'd made with Dan Curtis to return for *War and Remembrance*, which began filming in January 1986, with Hart Bochner as Byron Henry.

Television offers poured in for Jan—who had not worked in series television since *The Survivors*—after *The Winds of War*; they were from the networks and show creators, who were eager to capitalize on what they thought they'd seen in *The Winds of War*, which was Jan's rebirth.

He was a wanted man.

Part Four

The Defiant One

1984-1994

"We called him Jan-Michael Vodka."

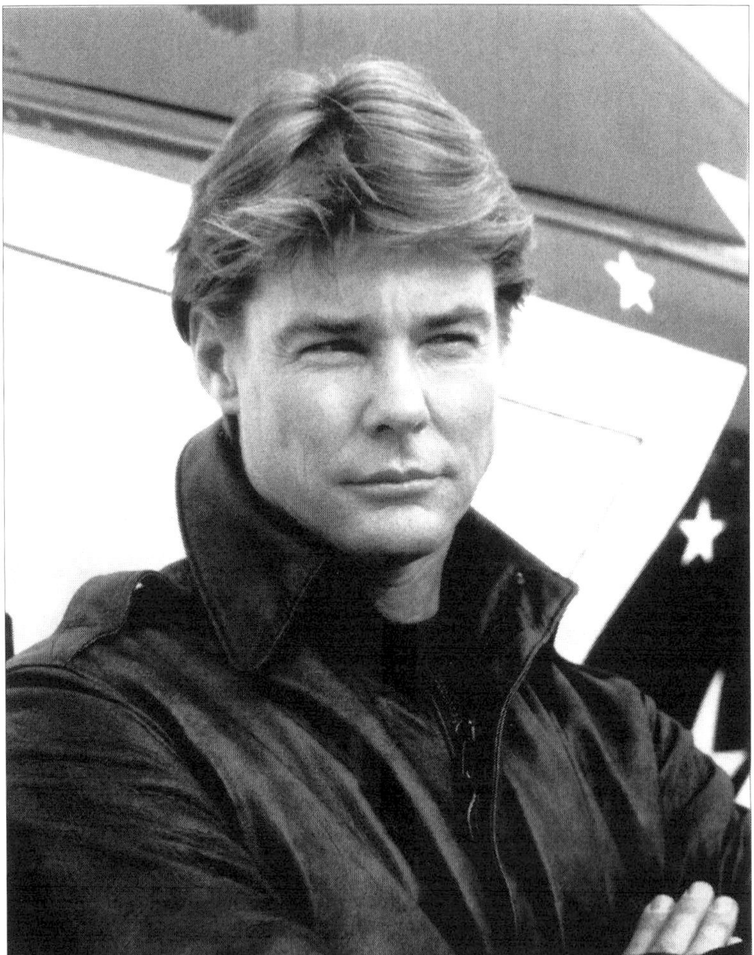

1
Undeserving

The aura created by television in the seventies and eighties was mercilessly short-lived, which was especially true of a miniseries like *The Winds of War*, whose running time severely limited the possibility of future broadcasts, foretelling a dim afterlife for the miniseries, which is exactly what has happened.

Jan's return to series television in the fall of 1983, when he began work on *Airwolf*, was just one of several transitions he went through between 1983 and 1984, all of which conspired to end his career.

There was Jan's divorce from Bonnie, who filed for divorce in April 1984, following an interminable separation. This, Jan knew, was inevitable, but the finality of losing Bonnie was devastating. He had, of course, been seeing countless women during the marriage and the separation, but in 1983, in advance of the divorce filing, Jan entered into his first serious post-Bonnie relationship, when he invited Joanne Robinson—an occasional model, a Malibu neighbor with deep roots in the community—to move into his one bedroom oceanfront house, which had become Jan's sanctuary ever since his separation from Bonnie in 1976.

Joanne, who had known Jan since the mid-1970s, when she was a teenager, was fully aware of Jan's appetites for alcohol and drugs and had taken Jan's confession regarding his many infidelities. She was—between 1983, with the triumph of *The Winds of War*, and their wedding in September 1986—the only living witness to the totality of Jan's destruction, which saw him first momentarily soar through the air, performing several crisp circles before he crashed to the earth, never to rise again, not even a little bit.

The only sign of trouble that seeped outside of Malibu to Hollywood in 1983, prior to Jan's casting in *Airwolf*, was when Jan was arrested and charged with two counts of drunk driving, to which he pleaded guilty in December 1983. He was given probation.

Hollywood was even more forgiving; Jan was courted, aggressively so, by CBS, *Airwolf*'s network, and by the series' production studio, Universal, where Jan's career had begun in 1966. Although Jan had not worked on the Universal lot, where much of *Airwolf* was shot, for several years, he was treated like a returning hero, a contract player who had taken full advantage of the knowledge given to him and made the most of his potential.

Airwolf, which is the name of the supersonic military helicopter that the series was built around, was created by Donald P. Bellisario, the co-creator of *Magnum, P.I.*, a series which had, by the time *Airwolf* made its debut in January 1984, accumulated over $200 million in syndication sales.

Airwolf was born out of a 1983 *Magnum, P.I.* episode, entitled "Two Birds of a Feather," (March 17, 1983) which featured an ace combat pilot. Bellisario wanted to turn this episode into a *Magnum* spinoff, titled *Birds of a Feather*. However, the project stalled at Universal, which wasn't convinced of the appeal of a helicopter-based series and was worried about the costs associated with a series that revolved around aerial sequences, a still-evolving filmmaking technique, which was extremely expensive and time-consuming.

It was the film *Blue Thunder* (1983)—an action-thriller about a police surveillance helicopter in Los Angeles, which was released by Columbia Pictures in May 1983—that communicated Bellisario's vision for *Airwolf*, an altered version of *Birds of a Feather*, far more effectively to Universal than Bellisario was able to articulate.

After toying with the idea of making a sequel to *Blue Thunder*, which was a modest box office success but did not turn a profit during its theatrical run because of its cost, Columbia decided instead to turn *Blue Thunder* into an eponymous television series, which was developed and produced directly opposite *Airwolf*, which Universal put into production in the summer of 1983.

In creating *Airwolf*, Bellisario did not intend, originally, to mold the series and its protagonist, Stringfellow Hawke, in the image of Jan, but it turned out that way because Jan turned out that way. A crackerjack helicopter pilot, a Vietnam veteran, Stringfellow Hawke is the ultimate loner; he lives in seclusion in a log cabin, which is located in a remote mountain area outside Los Angeles. There is no surfing here; he plays a Stradivarius cello and presides over a priceless collection of artwork; he hunts and reads and just wants to be left alone.

Such peace and solitude could not be allowed, for Jan, and for Hawke, who is brought out of hiding because of the titular helicopter, which Hawke, in the two hour pilot episode, retrieves from its demented creator, with the help of Dominic Santini, Stringfellow's partner and father figure. Santini is played by Oscar winner Ernest Borgnine, who assumed similar paternal responsibilities with Jan over the course of the series.

Stringfellow Hawke is no Thomas Magnum, though the elements of the chopper and Vietnam were common to both series, and *Magnum, P.I.*'s Hawaiian setting would've been a dream for Jan, who had stopped treating the surf in Hawaii as a form of rehab between acting assignments. Although the character of Thomas Magnum allowed for introspection and moodiness and moments of self-examination, the Magnum character was defined by his gregariousness and warmth, which were two of the many underrated qualities possessed by Tom Selleck, who was, in the tradition of Gary Cooper and Clark Gable, a big man who could be alternately gentle and tough.

Jan looked like a child alongside Selleck, who was at least six inches taller than Jan and was much further ahead of Jan than that in terms of the star lessons Selleck had received, and assimilated, during his long apprenticeship, most notably from James Garner, Selleck's mentor, who showed Selleck—both off screen, and when Selleck appeared in several episodes of Garner's *The Rockford Files*—how to captain a television series. Selleck wasn't only the star of *Magnum, P.I.*; he was the quarterback of the series, someone the cast and crew looked to for guidance and strength. Jan had never been into team sports.

When Bellisario first met Jan, he mistook Jan's moodiness and his increasingly dark, somber tone for Stringfellow Hawke, whose dimensions are not far removed from the characters Jan had played in *Baby Blue Marine* and especially *Tribes*, the two performances that were foremost in Bellisario's mind when he thought about Jan, whom Bellisario initially had no interest in working with. "I had heard that Jan was a heavy drinker before we did *Airwolf*, and I didn't want him," recalls Bellisario. "He didn't have a good reputation. It was the studio that insisted that I use Jan, and I went along with this, against my better judgment."

Ernest Borgnine became a father figure to Jan on the television series *Airwolf* but eventually grew tired of Jan's behavior.

Although Jan's grasp of acting and performing in front of the camera had declined considerably since his initial meeting with Dan Curtis in the fall of 1980, he had become a much more accomplished salesman, which is how Jan—whose base salary during *Airwolf*'s first season was $75,000 per episode, which increased to $100,000 in the second season and $125,000 in the third and final season—appeared to Bellisario throughout the summer of 1983.

The first meeting between Jan and Bellisario took place in Bellisario's bungalow on the Universal lot, which had formerly been occupied by Alfred Hitchcock, who might have appreciated the ruse that Jan, and his bulky entourage, pulled off. "Jan brought his entire team with him—there was his agent, his manager, his PR guy, even his doctor," recalls Bellisario. "They all took turns talking to me; they all told me that Jan wanted to change, and that he had changed, and that he'd gone to rehab and there would be no more drinking. I remember Jan just sitting there for that first meeting, while everyone was talking about him. He didn't say much at all."

There were no excuses for failure to be found in the production, which surrounded Jan with the most accommodating and stable support system he'd ever had, in or out of his career. Besides Bellisario, and Borgnine, whom Jan adored and became dependent on, Jan was reunited with Alex Cord, over a decade after they'd worked together in the 1973 *Police Story* episode "Line of Fire," the last time they'd spoken to each other prior to the start of filming on *Airwolf*.

Cord plays Archangel, the eye-patch wearing head of the Firm, a shadowy intelligence agency, a secret branch of the CIA, whom Hawke reluctantly agrees to perform missions for throughout the series in exchange for the Firm agreeing to help track down Hawke's older brother, St. John, who went missing in Vietnam. "I had not seen Jan since we'd worked together on the *Police Story* episode, but the camaraderie we'd shared was instantly restored," says Cord. "Jan looked great when we started, and there was a real feeling of optimism, from the entire cast and crew, about the future of the show and about Jan's performance. Jan and I were very happy to see each other again, and I did not know about Jan's drinking on *Airwolf*; I only recognized the similarities between Jan and my son, with their shared problems with drugs."

Ultimately, *Airwolf*, whose production budget of $1.2 million per episode made it the most expensive series on television at that time, belonged to Jan, and the Airwolf helicopter, which was represented throughout the series by a Bell 222 luxury helicopter, which was heavily modified for the series, at a cost of $1.5 million.

Jan was not capable of such heavy lifting; he provided a face behind the helicopter, which was the bare minimum that Bellisario required of him, and then even this proved to be too much for him. "Jan was in terrible shape during *Airwolf*, and they put too much responsibility on his shoulders," says Robert Englund. "Jan had to carry the show, which he was not capable of doing."

Jan, unsurprisingly, was at his best during the filming of the two hour pilot episode, entitled "Shadow of the Hawke," which was directed and written by Bellisario, very much in the pattern of a feature film, which is how the pilot was sold in some overseas markets. Bellisario was encouraged by Jan's early dedication to the role; Jan devoted two weeks to cello lessons and paid careful attention to the flight instructions he received from the series' aerial coordinator, David Jones, solely for the purpose of looking right in the cockpit, which became increasingly difficult throughout the first season. "When Jan wasn't drunk, he did a good job," says Bellisario. "Later on in the series, when things got really bad, we would have to put Jan in the cockpit, with his helmet on, and we'd let him sleep there. Ernie and the script girl would help Jan; Ernie did everything he could to help Jan but became disgusted with Jan after awhile."

Jan does well in the pilot episode; the only problem with his performance here is that it, like everything else in the series, pales in comparison to the aerial sequences, which dominate the pilot's third act and are completely arresting.

Bellisario was initially satisfied with Jan's performance, and his work ethic, which remained steady until the end of the pilot's filming, when Jan, who drank a quart of alcohol a day while on the series, started drinking.

"When we did the pilot, Jan was sober until the last day of filming, when he got drunk, which was obvious," says Bellisario. "If Jan had continued to perform the role as I'd written it for him, I think the show could've lasted much longer, and Jan could've had a successful second career in television going forward."

CBS aired the *Airwolf* pilot on January 22, 1984, following the broadcast of Super Bowl XVIII, which ensured a massive lead-in audience for the pilot, which did not turn out to be at all indicative of *Airwolf*'s ratings performance going forward. The pilot arrived just a few days after the debut of *Blue Thunder*, which aired on ABC and lasted eleven episodes before it was canceled in April.

The ratings of the remaining ten episodes from *Airwolf*'s abbreviated first season, the last of which aired on April 14, 1984, were stronger than those of *Blue Thunder* but hardly qualified *Airwolf*, which aired on Saturday night, as a hit. *Airwolf*'s ratings did not improve during the following two seasons, and neither did Jan's condition, though CBS's investment in the series, which ended up being north of $70 million, and in Jan, gave the series a longer leash than would've ordinarily existed and gave Jan a cloak of invincibility against any attempts to curtail his behavior and enforce some semblance of discipline over a production that increasingly resembled a junkyard.

Although Jan's performance in the first season's remaining episodes was functional and was considered entirely satisfactory by the network, the erratic pattern of Jan's drinking—which usually began at seven in the morning, in the oversized mobile home that was lavished upon him—threw the rest of the cast and crew off stride. "I couldn't work like that," says Bellisario, whose then wife, Deborah Pratt, an actress and writer, played the role of Marella, Archangel's assistant, in the first two seasons. "We had to write shows to deal with Jan's condition, which changed from episode to episode, which created a lack of continuity. When Jan was sober, we would have to reshoot scenes."

Production on the first season ended in March 1984, which was followed by a lengthy hiatus, over four months, before production on the second season started in August. Bellisario saw an opportunity here; he wanted to send Jan to rehab before Jan resumed filming on the second season. "I wanted Jan to go into rehab after the first season," says Bellisario. "The studio, Universal, wouldn't even consider this and gave me no support in terms of dealing with Jan."

2
Encore

He was also a victim.

In April 1984, Jan was vacationing in Kauai and was lounging around the pool area of the resort hotel he was staying at when he was approached by a burly man, an ornery Texan, who asked Jan to punch him. Jan refused and received a cut on his chin in the resulting melee, where a friend of Jan's struck the man, who was arrested and charged with third degree assault.

On June 3, 1984, Jan, who was gearing up for the second season of *Airwolf*, visited the Trancas Restaurant, his then favorite watering hole in Malibu, late one night after receiving a call from a friend. While Jan was standing near the bar, attempting to acquire change for a nearby cigarette machine, he was approached, from behind, by John Bogosian, a six-foot-two man who recognized Jan immediately and clearly wasn't a fan.

Bogosian—according to Jan, in his court testimony—shoved Jan several times and told Jan he was standing in a place reserved for Bogosian's female companion that night, who later testified that Bogosian, who weighed over 210 pounds at the time, had consumed at least eight tequilas—each of which was followed by a beer—in less than an hour.

Bogosian, according to Jan, threw a looping, sloppy punch, which Jan blocked and returned with a punch of his own, a single uppercut, which was apparently enough to leave Bogosian unconscious and put him in intensive care for several days, which was the reason, probably the only reason, why

Jan was charged with misdemeanor battery. The trial, which lasted three days, took place in May 1985 and resulted in an acquittal for Jan, which, in this case, was the same as being innocent.

Jan, it must be said, never thought he was better than the people who supported him and put him in the position he was in.

During the *Airwolf* period, Jan befriended several children from the Make-A-Wish Foundation; he went to see them in the hospital and invited them to Universal City to watch the filming. Their courage and perseverance touched Jan's heart; this drove him to tears and highlighted, for him and everyone who saw them together, how little Jan had made of his many advantages.

Item: One episode in the second season required a group of paraplegics to participate in the filming of a wheelchair race that Hawke watches over. Jan was so drunk that he could barely stand up and match the eyelevel of the paraplegics, who were quite dismayed by the sight of him. "One of the paraplegics pointed at Jan and said something like, 'He's the one who looks handicapped—he's the one who needs a wheelchair,'" recalls Bellisario. "I'll never forget that."

With Universal unwilling to adopt Bellisario's suggestion to put Jan into rehab and hit pause on the series, several changes were made in advance of *Airwolf*'s second season, in reaction to Jan's behavior and the disappointing ratings during the abbreviated first season.

The international flavor of the first season was abandoned in favor of turning *Airwolf* into a domestic adventure series in its second season, not far removed from *Magnum, P.I.*—it was now going to be *Magnum* in the air. No one said that, but the implication was obvious. Actress Jean Bruce Scott, who had appeared opposite Tom Selleck on *Magnum, P.I.*, joined *Airwolf*'s cast in the role of Caitlin O'Shannessy, a feisty former Texas Highway Patrol helicopter pilot who joins Airwolf's crew for the purpose of being a potential love interest for Hawke.

With Stringfellow Hawke, Bellisario took away his cello, the ultimate symbol of Hawke's glumness, and suggested to Jan that he might want to smile more in the second season. These were modest changes and requests, which had the full of support of Jan, who pledged, in press interviews that were conducted during the hiatus, to give more to the show the second time around, admitting that he'd shortchanged the show, and himself, during the first season.

It appears, from the accounts of the cast and crew, that this gesture of goodwill lasted no more than two episodes. Jan became increasingly isolated;

he stayed inside the mobile home for three or four hours at a time, holding up production routinely. He tried, as best he could, to turn the mobile home into a replica of his crash party pad on the Malibu shore and invited many of the same people to join him—Gary Busey was a regular visitor. "Jan showed some self-awareness of his situation, when I went to visit him on the set of *Airwolf*," says Dennis Aaberg. "He said, 'If I took care of myself, I could have a career like Robert Wagner's.' There was too much drinking, and there were too many parties; Jan was in that party group with Gary and Nick Nolte, and others, all of them doing cocaine. Jan was never able to stop."

There were changes in Jan's behavior. Jan's drink of choice had changed from Heineken to the Sea Breeze vodka-based cocktails he consumed every morning before the start of filming. "Jan felt like he didn't deserve the success he had," says Aaberg. "When Jan was doing *Airwolf*, he was getting drunk every day, and he started to look bad physically; he was starting to show the wear, which I could see, from the drinking and the drugs; he was starting to get bloated. He would be in his trailer, drinking sea breezes with vodka, and he had to be propped up. Ernest Borgnine got very angry with Jan over time, because Ernest was a professional."

His sexual behavior became increasingly deviant and sordid; he wanted two women, then three women, and then he only wanted to watch. Joanne later complained of being debased and degraded as a woman by his requests, which did not stop her from wholeheartedly agreeing to marry him.

In August 1984, Joanne accompanied Jan to Catalina Island for the filming of the episode entitled "Sins of the Past" (October 27, 1984) and ended up breaking Jan's right arm, an injury that is visible in this episode, and in the following episode, "Fallen Angel," (November 3, 1984) where Jan, who is right-handed, is forced to grab the helicopter's controls and door with his left hand. Neither the injury to his arm nor his worsening relationship with Joanne kept him out of action long.

The broken arm happened on Catalina Island after Joanne had fled their hotel room, after she had awakened and seen Jan standing over her, next to a young man, who was naked and stroking a full erection. This beautiful young man was a gift from Jan, who told Joanne he wanted to watch them have sex—he only wanted to watch, though Jan and the young man both leapt onto the bed, while Joanne excused herself by saying she needed to go to the washroom.

She tried to escape instead; she reached for the sliding glass door but was blocked by Jan, who, according to Joanne, punched her in her side. She broke free of Jan, and then she slammed the door on Jan's right arm on her way outside, where Joanne, who was naked, was discovered by a cop in a police car, who gave her a blanket and ushered her over to a helicopter pad, where Joanne's face and neck nearly made direct contact with the blades of a chopper.

Jan's only confidante on *Airwolf* was his stunt double, Reid Rondell, whom Jan had first gotten to know when they worked together on *Hooper*, when Reid was a teenager. Despite the age difference, Jan considered Reid a best friend and the bravest man he had ever met. They shared a daredevil mindset and a love of helicopters, and Reid was one of the few people Jan truly admired.

Because Reid was nearly twenty years younger than Jan, this was the first professional relationship of Jan's in which he filled the role of father figure or older brother, though Jan had partied with Reid, who was only twenty-two on January 18, 1985, when he was killed. "Jan and Reid were very close," recalls Alex Cord. "We were all devastated by Reid's passing but Jan especially. I don't think he ever got over it."

Jan was not present for the helicopter crash that took Reid's life; Jan was drunk and out of commission when the Bell 205 helicopter Reid was riding in, in the backseat, crashed and burned on a hillside near Newhall, about twenty-five miles north of Los Angeles, not far from the site where actor Vic Morrow and two children were killed by a helicopter during the making of the film *Twilight Zone: The Movie* (1983). "I was involved in the investigation and found that everyone on *Airwolf*—everyone who was with Jan—was on dope," says stuntman Kim Kahana, Jan's former costar and friend. "It was not a good environment on that show, and Jan was going crazy, though he was nowhere around when the crash took place."

The Bell 205 was being used for a chase sequence for the episode entitled "Natural Born," (February 23, 1985) which was dedicated to Rondell's memory. Two helicopters were active for the sequence, and the one Rondell was in was set to make its third pass through a canyon, when the helicopter collided with the hilly, rolling terrain it was circling at a low altitude, the helicopter descending in its final turn, instead of leveling off, as it had done so many times before. "We had done hundreds of flying sequences and never had a problem," says Bellisario. "It was just a tragic accident, and there was no reason to blame Jan—him being there or not being there —for anything that happened that day."

Immediately after impact, David Jones, *Airwolf*'s aerial coordinator, and several other crew members, raced to the helicopter to try and save their comrades. Jones was able to pull the pilot out of the burning helicopter but could not save Rondell, who was pinned under the engine and was, mercifully, unconscious when the fire took him. "Reid Rondell's death really destroyed Jan," says Robert Englund. "I think it pushed him over the edge."

Rondell, who came from a family of stunt performers, was beloved by everyone who had worked with him; Tom Cruise, whom Rondell had doubled for several times, was disconsolate at the news and immediately flew back from England, where he was filming *Legend* (1985), to serve as one of Rondell's pallbearers, alongside Jan, who had never been hit so hard by tragedy and no longer wanted to live.

None of the changes made during the second season worked.

The ratings did not improve, and *Airwolf* was plagued by production cost overruns, which translated into millions of dollars in losses for Universal, which saw little recoupment of its investment in the syndication market, where *Airwolf*—which lasted for fifty-five episodes on CBS, far short of the total that's usually required for a successful syndication run and sale—was treated like a white elephant.

Gigi Jeffers, a Malibu stuntwoman, was hired to babysit Jan; her job was to make sure he was straight during filming. She was not successful; much of the footage with Jan throughout the second season was horrible, requiring extraordinary measures in post-production just to make the scenes usable. The addition of Jean Bruce Scott, who was beloved by the entire cast and crew, did not stir Jan or lead to the hoped for fireworks between her character and Stringfellow Hawke, whose romantic relationships, like Jan's, always ended in tragedy.

Donald Bellisario, unhappy with the show's direction and frustrated at the lack of support he was receiving from Universal in regards to dealing with Jan, left the show and the studio at the end of the second season, which also meant the departure of costar Deborah Pratt, Bellisario's then wife. "The last straw for me, with Jan, was when one of the grips came to me one day and told me that Jan was asking him for syringes," says Bellisario. "I could not deal with Jan anymore, and that's why I left."

3
Point of No Return

Throughout 1985, Jan believed that he would be included in the miniseries *War and Remembrance*, the sequel to *The Winds of War*, even though *War and Remembrance*'s filming, which began in early 1986, was destined to conflict with the filming of *Airwolf*'s third and final season. He thought he was an indispensable ingredient.

To Jan, and his crumbling group of supporters, *War and Remembrance* was a hedge against the imminent collapse of *Airwolf* and the lurid, wild stories that were leaking out from Universal City about Jan, about a cancer that was not only incurable but also untreatable. "I was filming the *New Leave It to Beaver* television series on the Universal lot while *Airwolf* was in production, and there were lots of stories about Jan spreading around the studio and Hollywood," says Tony Dow, Jan's costar from *Lassie*. "I had not seen Jan in many years, but when I heard about his behavior, I thought about how unhappy he'd always seemed when we were together, which I took, in retrospect, to be depression and a pain that no one could understand."

Scheduling was a legitimate reason for Jan being left out of *War and Remembrance*, as was age, which was the reason why Ali MacGraw was replaced in the nearly thirty hour sequel by the younger Jane Seymour, though MacGraw had, unquestionably, been *The Winds of War*'s weakest link. However, these obstacles would not have been at all insurmountable if Dan Curtis had wanted Jan back, which was not the case.

Hart Bochner, Jan's replacement, could not have been more different from Jan. Bochner, the son of veteran character actor Lloyd Bochner, was dark-haired and several inches taller than Jan, and he was infinitely more controllable. Bochner, whose rosy-cheeked handsomeness was concealed inside the shape of a general purpose actor, also cost much less than Jan, though Jan's salary requirements played little role in Curtis' decision-making regarding the sequel, whose eventual production cost topped $100 million.

It will never be known how much Jan was capable of giving to *War and Remembrance* and what effect, if any, his presence would've had on the miniseries, whose twelve episodes aired, on a staggered basis, between November 1988 and May 1989. Nor can any comparison be made between Jan and Bochner, who is more than a decade younger than Jan and only carried modest potential for stardom, which was not realized.

War and Remembrance was a failure compared to *The Winds of War*; the ratings for the sequel were down sharply, which Curtis blamed, not unreasonably, on the non-sequential airings. ABC ended up posting a loss of nearly $40 million, which no one blamed on Jan—or the lack of him.

Airwolf should've been canceled after its second season but was deemed too expensive to end at this point—prior to its threshold for syndication—by CBS, and especially by Universal, which ended up posting a $12 million loss on *Airwolf* over the three seasons.

This meant that Jan's presence at Universal City, reviled as it was at this point by the cast and crew and Universal executives, was entirely necessary, and Jan—in a repeat of how he had entered the filming of the second season—arrived on the Universal lot in August looking rested and tanned.

He looked terrific, which was encouraging to Bernard Kowalski, who took over from Donald Bellisario as the series' executive producer and made even fewer demands of Jan, who had spent two weeks of the three month hiatus sailing in Mexico on a thirty-two foot Ericson sloop Jan claimed after it had sunk off the coast of Ventura.

Jan had not been arrested during the hiatus, a streak that was broken very early in the third season's filming schedule, in September 1985, when Jan was charged with a count of felony battery after allegedly striking Chenoa Lee Ellis, a female acquaintance of Jan's, in the face at his Malibu residence.

Ellis, who suffered a broken nose, and a split lip that required several stitches, said that Jan had struck her after accusing her of causing a rift in Jan's relationship with Joanne, while Jan countered that he had never touched Ellis, who had, according to Jan, become enraged at Jan after Jan refused to have sex with her.

At his trial, which began in July 1986, Jan testified that it was this rejection that prompted Ellis to slap Jan, who said that Ellis then tripped over a telephone cord, knocked over a planter, then cut her lip on a door frame, a story that was supported by the physical evidence found at the scene—the blood-smeared door frame. Jan was acquitted in October by a jury, several of whom later requested autographs from Jan, who had tears running down his face as he left the courtroom.

Airwolf's final episode, "Birds of Paradise," (March 29, 1986) finished filming in March 1986, just a few weeks before it aired, and there was little will from the cast and crew to continue with Jan, who was arrested for driving under the influence of alcohol in Ventura County on May 15, a violation of Jan's December 1983 conviction on two counts of drunk driving.

He was sentenced to thirty days in jail, which was stayed and then lifted when Jan agreed to enter an alcohol treatment program.

In June, CBS announced that *Airwolf* would not be back in the fall, citing poor ratings.

4
Falling Down

The wedding of Jan and Joanne was Jan's second marriage but his first formal ceremony, which was entirely a differentiation without a difference. The lavish outdoor ceremony took place on September 1, 1986, at Montecito Valley Ranch, eighty miles northwest of Los Angeles, with over 300 guests in attendance: There was Doris and Lloyd, who were now living in Montana; Christopher was Jan's best man; thirteen-year-old Amber was a bridesmaid; there were several of the crippled children Jan had befriended; Gary Busey and David Carradine headlined the modest celebrity contingent.

The wedding was a production, sponsored by the *National Enquirer*, which was supposed to lay the groundwork for a comeback. However, Jan lacked the desire for an attempted comeback, and there were large questions about his remaining talent, which had not revealed itself, in any prolonged burst, in nearly a decade. Hollywood, of course, loves comebacks but loathes flea markets.

He did not arrive at the wedding unscathed; several of his toes had become swollen after a surfing mishap, which left him unable to fill his dress shoes. Jan was in his socks when he exchanged vows with Joanne, which were not at all spontaneous, as when he married Bonnie in Acapulco during the filming of *Danger Island*. He did fall into tears the second time. "I visited Jan in Topanga after *Airwolf*, and it looked to me like he was gone," says Jonathan Kaplan. "He was drinking and taking drugs; he was doing smack. I tried to sit with him, but he was all fucked up. I think he had brain damage as time went on, and I believe that he lost his will to live."

Jan returned to acting in October, when he filmed a guest spot on the television series *Hotel*, a series that focused on the guests and happenings at an elegant, fictitious hotel in San Francisco. *Hotel*, which ran from 1983 to 1988, was basically *Love Boat* in a hotel, and the types of actors who appeared on the show were remarkably similar— they were all desperate, on the way down, or out, all lost.

Mary Crosby, Marilyn Hassett, Martin Landau, Don Stroud—former costars of Jan's—all guest-starred on *Hotel*, which offered the refuge that *Love Boat* did to has-beens but specialized more in dispossessed souls like Jan, who was dimly aware of the need to show himself on camera in a positive light following the end of *Airwolf* and the resulting bad publicity.

In "Undercurrents," a fourth season episode that aired in November 1986, Jan appears as Nick Hauser, an army officer who checks into the hotel with his buddy, Rodger Gage, played by Boyd Gaines, for a fun weekend on the town. After Rodger is assaulted by street punks in a gay neighborhood, following a romantic rendezvous with his gay lover, Nick is forced to confront the fact that his friend is a homosexual, which is not something that Nick—who was raised to believe in conservative, traditional family values—is able to deal with. Nick later defends his friend against the same attacking gang but is, finally, unable to accept his friend's orientation, which is not, in all likelihood, the choice that would have been made by Jan, who was liberal on social issues but also a closet Republican.

Then he returned to *Airwolf*.

Jan was not, as it turned out, finished with the character of Stringfellow Hawke, although the feeling certainly wasn't mutual on the part of CBS and Universal, which were just two of Hollywood's major entities to have scribbled Jan's name into the pages of their black books with red ink.

In the fall of 1986, Universal, in a last-ditch attempt to reduce its loss on *Airwolf* and to bolster the series' prospects in the syndication market, entered into a partnership with Atlantis Films, a Canadian production company, which intended to produce additional episodes of *Airwolf* for cable television's USA Network.

The Canadian producers reached out to Ernest Borgnine and Alex Cord, although the new series, which lasted a total of twenty-four episodes, operated on a drastically reduced budget compared to its predecessor—the budget of this reincarnation was roughly $400,000 per episode, which allowed few luxuries, including the helicopter, which was presented via stock footage.

Borgnine refused to even consider the idea, and neither Cord nor Jan showed any interest when they were first contacted. "After the end of *Airwolf* at Universal, the next time I spoke to Jan was when they were doing the new low budget series in Canada and wanted me and Jan and Ernest to be in it," says Cord. "I read the pilot script, which I thought was very poor. When I spoke to Jan, he also told me that he didn't like it, and we both agreed that we weren't going to be a part of it. I guess Jan changed his mind, because he had to prove to the industry that he was still alive and viable."

In November, Jan traveled to Vancouver, British Columbia, to film the first episode of the new series, which acted as a bridge between the CBS series and this version. He was, according to those involved with the production, cheerful and entirely professional, and he later cut a promotional advertisement for the series, which aired on the USA Network between January and August of 1987.

Jan's role in the episode could not have been less demanding if his character was in a coma, which is what happens very early on in the new series, after Hawke is critically injured. His eventual fate is left up in the air.

5
Video Killed the Film Star

He still had friends.

These were not the enablers, who continue to maintain a shadowy presence in his life, but rather the loyal friends who had nothing to gain from him. When they finally walked away from him, it was not out of anger or disgust but as a form of preemptive grief.

One of Jan's most loyal friends was comedic actor Richard "Cheech" Marin, who was one half, with Thomas Chong, of the coarse comedy team Cheech & Chong, who appeared in a series of hippy-themed comedy films, which found a loyal but capped audience in the early to mid-1980s. "Jan and Cheech were friends, and Cheech also tried to help Jan," says mutual friend Jonathan Kaplan. "The three of us used to frequent this great barbecue grill restaurant in Trancas, and Cheech and I went there together one day, thinking we might run into Jan. On our way inside, we walked past this pickup truck, whose cab looked like it had been set on fire; the front was burned, as if the owner had totaled it and been in a horrible accident and been seriously hurt. We found Jan inside, sipping a drink, his voice gravelly; he looked like he was trying to kill himself. He asked us if we'd seen the new pickup truck he'd bought. We told him we thought it looked nice."

In early 1987, Marin was preparing to make his directorial debut with the film *Born in East L.A.*, Marin's first without Chong, which Marin had placed at Universal, which only put up mild resistance when Marin revealed his intention to cast Jan in a lead role, which ended up being an exaggerated cameo.

Jan was supposed to play the film's villain, whom Marin, the writer, named McAlister—the unconventional spelling is the character's only distinguishing feature. He only appears in one scene, early in the film. This is all that Marin—Marin the director, not Jan's friend—surmised that Jan was capable of during the brief, disastrous rehearsals that Jan stumbled through in front of Marin in March 1987, just prior to the start of filming.

Jan plays a sadistic immigration officer who is responsible for deporting Marin's character early in the film. In the scene, which takes place in a factory that is crawling with undocumented workers, Jan—whose hyper manner had to be neutralized by covering his eyes with dark, oversized glasses to go with the Texas Ranger's hat he wore on his head—storms through the factory, mumbles his few, truncated lines of dialogue and then disappears from the film.

Rigorous editing in post-production—the vicious cutting of Jan that was required to account for and to try and match his ragged movements and slurred speech—and Marin's unrewarded benevolence were the only factors that kept Jan in the film, and even then he appears as the residue of a botched filmmaking procedure, left behind, for no good reason.

Clearly, this did not warrant the fourth billing Jan received in the film, which was another good-natured but shambling and thin effort from Marin, indistinguishable from his prior Cheech & Chong films, including at the box office, where *Born in East L.A.* placed strongly in its opening weekend and then fell sharply afterward.

Jan is credited in the film beneath Paul Rodriguez, a comedic actor who interviewed Jan on his late night talk show in August 1987, when *Born in East L.A.* was released, and Daniel Stern, who assumed the rest of Jan's responsibilities and provides the film's few comedic highlights as a slimy immigrant smuggler. The only silver lining here was that Jan was already too damaged for his non-performance in the film, his last appearance in a studio film, to have done more harm than good. It didn't change anything.

Jan's fall from the mainstream, his complete loss of dignity, was, by 1987, primarily documented by tabloid reporters, who followed him during the squalid nights he spent at the gold-crusted ghettos in Malibu. He was flattered by this attention, while he punched and kicked them.

One of Jan's favorite haunts in Malibu was the Dume Room, a notorious dive bar, tucked between a dry cleaning store and a pizza parlor, whose patrons were mostly faded wonder boys from the 1970s who were no longer able to find work.

There was still work for Jan; there was so much embarrassing, horrible work, which is not the same as working. It was—to paraphrase a line from *Hard Country* that was spoken not by Jan but actor Michael Parks—a whore's game, and he did it for the money. "I did not see Jan for many years, and then I ran into him outside my favorite watering hole in Laguna Beach," says Robert Englund. "We saw each other, and I thought, from afar, that he looked great. As I got closer and closer to him, he looked worse and worse. His teeth were rotted."

Jan's transition to the straight-to-video market in the late 1980s was very ungraceful, even by the bargain basement standards of an industry built around the premise of plucking reclamation projects like Jan from Hollywood's funeral pyre and then dumping them onto the cable television channels and the video store shelves.

Jan appeared in nine of these films between 1987 and 1990—*Enemy Territory* (1987), *Hit List* (1987), *Deadly Embrace* (1989), *Dirty Games* (1989), *In Gold We Trust* (1990), *Alienator* (1990), *Deathstone* (1990), *Haunting Fear* (1990), *Xtro II: The Second Encounter* (1990)—and over a dozen more through 1994, the year Jan turned fifty. "I think the story of Jan's career, in terms of why he never reached major stardom, was that he had bad management and ended up choosing projects not for the quality but the money that was being offered," says Jonathan Kaplan. "I went to visit Leo Rossi, a friend of mine, and Jan, when they were shooting a low budget movie together called *Hit List*. Jan had trouble walking from his trailer to the set and had to be helped and had to be given his lines. He was all gone, but when he saw me, he smiled and said, 'I've still got the balls; I've still got the voice.'"

The name was now worth far more than the man, and the price was $100,000, Jan's established salary between 1987 and 1995. He accepted his role within the home video wasteland; he made appearances at the conventions, where he schmoozed with the distributors and retailers and signed autographs. The filming schedules resembled episodic television but were far less rigid; he could make five films a year. He did not have to do pornography, though several of the films he appeared in were thinly-veiled exercises in soft-core, disguised as psychological thrillers. It was easy work that should've provided some level of contentment.

Jan in 1992. (Photo courtesy of Steve Fenton www.brokentreaty.com)

Doris died on February 22, 1993, at the age of sixty-seven, in Tulare, Lloyd's birthplace. "Jan changed slowly for the worse after his mother died," says Rudy Ramos. "He loved his mother and father, but he took her death very hard. He was, like when he was doing *Airwolf*, in no shape to be working and was crying out for help with his behavior."

Jan's marriage to Joanne was turbulent and violent, according to the restraining order that Joanne filed against Jan in November 1994, in which she accused him of beating her, causing black eyes and broken ribs, forcing her to engage in group sex, and stomping her kitten to death. Jan was ordered to stay 300 yards away from Joanne—who filed for divorce in December—and their Malibu oceanfront residence, which drove Jan into the Valley, where he stayed with a friend for several months.

Also in November, Jan—who had started work on a film called *Red Line* (1995), an action film with Michael Madsen, Dom DeLuise, and Steve McQueen's son, Chad McQueen—was driving in a 1993 Ford Bronco one night along Encinal Canyon Road, when the Bronco slammed straight into a wall. Jan—whose face went through the windshield, which left him with a detached retina, causing temporary blindness in his right eye—was airlifted to the nearest hospital, where his badly scarred face—which necessitated a hasty reworking of *Red Line*'s script to account for this—was stitched up.

He returned to the set the next morning.

Part Five

The One Take Wonder

1995-2017

"It's a major tragedy."

(Photo courtesy of Jeff Minton/Corbis Images)

Nothing more needs to be said.

In 1995, Jan toyed with the idea of writing his autobiography, which was going to be titled *The Best Dirt Road I Ever Lived On*, which was Jan's description of his life, mostly his life in Malibu, which had, by this point, eclipsed Jan's existence in Hanford by a lifetime.

He was motivated to do a book by the money, of course, his finances exhausted by two divorces and continuous legal bills. A publishing contract was hastily arranged, which Jan was unable to consummate. It turned out he was sterile.

He discovered this in April 1995, during a medical examination, which he had undergone as part of an attempt to fight a woman's claim that he had beaten her and caused her to suffer a spontaneous miscarriage.

He denied this. He denied that he had ever beaten a woman; he denied beating Joanne and killing her beloved kitten. He denied shooting heroin between his toes. He denied ever being homeless and panhandling on the beach. He admitted to being an alcoholic but said that this only took hold of him when he was thirty-five.

There were colorful stories to whet the appetite of the tabloids: the lessons in hard alcohol that he claimed he received from Lee Marvin, Robert Mitchum, John Wayne; there was his recounting of an alleged confrontation with Manson family enforcer Charles "Tex" Watson, whom Jan claimed —during Jan's early surf rat period in Malibu—he once pummeled on the beach after discovering that Watson had disfigured a horse Jan was fond of.

He spoke of a brief period in the 1970s, when he shared a house with legendary rockers Mick Jagger and Neil Young. He claimed to have an affiliation with the Hell's Angels, who, according to Jan, let Jan ride alongside them on several occasions and presented him with their hallowed One Percent badge. He mixed lies with the truth, which is not the same as engaging in publicity hype.

He had prepared headlines for every section of his life: In Hanford, there was the story of Clifford Vincent, one of Jan's uncles and a convicted bank robber and counterfeiter in his own right, whom Jan's grandfather, Herbert, according to Jan, believed to be a snitch after several cousins were put in jail on account of Clifford's supposedly big, loose mouth.

The story ended with Herbert handing a pistol to Clifford, which Clifford placed in his mouth. The way Jan told the story clearly gave the impression that Clifford—who had relocated to Washington State by the time Jan moved to Hanford—was expected to blow his own brains out as punishment for this transgression.

Jan said that he had belonged to a black gang as a teenager in Hanford, whose black population at that time, which was entrenched but small, lived quietly and mostly separately from the rest of Hanford. His former colleagues and friends from Hanford say this is ridiculous.

He is the least reliable witness in his own story.

Although Jan made little progress with his autobiography, he wrote some more songs, one of which he was heard singing while lying on his back after the crash along Encinal Canyon Road in November 1994. After the 1994 accident, he also scribbled an outline for a sequel to *Big Wednesday*, which he hoped to show to Dennis Aaberg and John Milius, who were, unbeknownst to Jan, interested instead in doing a *Big Wednesday* spinoff television series.

The television project started to take shape in the summer of 1996, while Jan was still busy churning out the straight-to-video titles—five were released in 1995, three more in 1996. "John and I were working on a television spinoff of *Big Wednesday*, which would've been a starring vehicle for Jan, playing an older Matt Johnson," says Aaberg. "It would've been in the vein of *Happy Days*, but when Jan got into the car accident, and he damaged his back and throat, John dropped out, and the whole thing fell apart."

Prior to the August 1996 car crash that broke his neck and made it difficult for him to continue working as an actor from then on, Jan had been living in Irvine, California, a fairly exclusive city in Orange County, in a small condominium that belonged to Karen Thompson, one of Jan's few female friends. "Karen Thompson was a very lovely lady," says Nick Miranda, who assumed the role of Jan's manager in 1997. "She was educated, cultured, everything Jan was not. She always cared for him more than he cared for her."

This relationship, which was intimate at the beginning but mostly platonic from then on, was separate from the stream of twenty-something, self-employed actresses and models Jan continued to attract. "Jan lived with her [Karen], not vice versa," says Miranda. "She always expressed her concerns and affection for Jan and regretted that she could not do more to make him change his ways. He cost her lots of money and caused emotional anguish; she was quite relieved when he left to move to Santa Monica."

Thompson, whom Jan described as a childhood friend, has roots in the San Joaquin Valley, though they never attended school together, and she became as much a sister to him as a romantic partner during their relationship, which ended in the fall of 1999, when Thompson asked Jan to leave, after Jan resumed his heavy drinking.

Karen was the president of Jan's mobile, entirely virtual fan club, and then, after the crash, she became his caregiver, which is her current occupation, this experience the only reward she gained from the relationship. "He was always totally flat broke," says Miranda. "I paid for everything—every time we went out for meals or for any events we attended. I also gave him money for cigarettes, and for gas, for a car he didn't even own—he drove Karen Thompson's car."

The August 1996 car crash could have provided the much-needed ending this life story was searching for, but it turned out to be just another turning point, a minor observation compared to where he is now. The crash itself yielded more positive effects than negative, not the least of which was the hastening of the end of his video career, which was no way for a grown man to make a living.

On August 26, 1996, Jan—who had a blood alcohol level of .18 when he arrived at Mission Hospital Regional Medical Center, where he remained for three weeks—was out in Mission Viejo, a city in Orange County, driving a 1988 Mazda, when the vehicle rear-ended the 1985 Cadillac he'd given to Nicole Wallace, a girlfriend of Jan's, who had her two sons, then aged five and six, in the car with her when Jan crashed into the Cadillac as she slowed to make a turn. Jan's car then spun out of control and hit a light pole; the impact snapped his neck.

After Jan, who was unconscious, was taken to the hospital, he was placed in the intensive care unit, where it was immediately determined that he had suffered a fractured second cervical vertebra, though a diagnosis of paralysis was ruled out two days later, when Jan, who had only slight movement in certain toes when he first awakened, demonstrated that he was able to move both of his feet and was quickly moving all of his extremities, while a steel halo, studded with bolts and screws, encircled his skull.

The accident almost certainly saved his life—there was the untreated brain damage, the epilepsy, pneumonia, and Jan's liver, whose failure, whose multiple deaths and reincarnations, briefly caused Jan to enter a coma. "My dog Jessie and I went to the hospital to visit Jan for the day," says Rudy Ramos. "The hospital let me take him outside; Jan had a halo screwed into his skull, so we couldn't go far off of the grounds without being noticed. He was in a good frame of mind and grateful to be alive but was very sad. He told me that none of his friends had come to visit him and no one had called except me and a reporter from the *National Enquirer*."

In September 1996, Jan—who had been driving with a suspended license, a result of the 1994 crash, where Jan was found to have a blood alcohol level of .33—was charged with one count of driving with a suspended license and two counts of drunken driving.

He had moved from the hospital to a rehab center, watched over by his brother, Christopher, and Karen Thompson, who eventually took custody of Jan and returned him to her condominium in Orange County, where he convalesced and contemplated the resumption of his acting career. "There was still a lot of pushback from casting directors and producers," says Miranda. "They just didn't want to have anything to do with him—he was considered poison."

His voice was almost inaudible; it was painful for him to talk and even more so for anyone else to listen to him and watch him strain. He blamed the trauma to his vocal chords not on the accident but the paramedics who treated him at the crash scene, whom he claimed, in his 1997 lawsuit, did not follow the proper life-saving protocol when they shoved a breathing tube down his throat.

He had little contact, during this period, with Amber, who was approaching her mid-twenties and working as a waitress in Los Angeles. "She was civil but distant, almost dismissive, as if to say, 'Good luck. You're going to need it,'" says Miranda. "The poor kid has had a tumultuous relationship with the one person who should have been her champion but wasn't. In conversations I had with Jan about Amber, he always did convey the impression that their relationship was contentious, which he readily admitted was his fault and directly related to his losing battle with the bottle. On a couple of occasions, I could see the lament on his face, because he appeared to love his daughter, yet because of his constant pickled state was just unable to communicate with her."

It is hard, mostly because of the disparate relationship between Jan's appearance and his age, to identify a figure, in show business, whose story is comparable to Jan's. The closest match is probably Ken Wahl, a dark-haired actor, for whom major film stardom was predicted in the late 1970s, the parallels to Jan, who is about ten years older than Wahl, separated by roughly five years. By the mid-1980s, Wahl's film career—after nondescript flops like *The Soldier* (1982), *Jinxed!* (1982), and *Purple Hearts* (1984)—had bottomed out, which put him in the same position that Jan was in at the end of the 1970s.

Wahl—following in Jan's footsteps, around the time of *The Winds of War*—turned to television, where he found minor stardom on the acclaimed crime-drama series *Wiseguy*, which aired on CBS and brought Wahl an Emmy nomination and a Golden Globe award for his work on the series, which he starred in from 1987 to 1990, when he walked away. In 1992, Wahl suffered a broken neck and spinal column injury in a fall down a staircase. He only acted twice more thereafter.

It was worth a try.

The few acting roles Jan received between 1997 and 1999 were entirely the result of charity. In 1997, Don Johnson and Cheech Marin, friends of Jan's, invited Jan to make a guest-starring appearance—which, for Jan, meant an extended cameo—on their television series *Nash Bridges*, which aired on CBS from 1996 to 2001.

In the episode entitled "Revelations," which aired in November 1997, Jan plays Johnson's long-lost older brother, who was thought to be a Vietnam MIA but is now living in San Francisco and suspected of being involved in a string of murders. "After securing the gig for Jan on *Nash Bridges* with his old friend, Don Johnson, I received a call from Johnson's office, asking me about Jan's condition," says Miranda. "I told the truth—Jan had to be watched or he would wander off and into a saloon. I hired a twenty-four hour bodyguard for Jan—a would-be groupie who was always hanging around him—with specific instructions to call me if he ever lost sight of Jan."

Jan filmed his scene, his only scene in the episode, from behind a screen, which was done to hide his features, which were heavily drawn. "Jan spoke in a hushed whisper, which was actually his natural voice by that time," says Miranda. "At three in the morning, after he arrived in San Francisco for the shooting, the bodyguard called me. Jan had wandered away; after walking the streets for several hours, he [the bodyguard] finally found him—in a saloon! After that, all went well; Jan finished the shoot in two days and returned to Los Angeles with no further incidents."

Although Jan's only scene—which was hazily-lit, another accommodation that was made in response to Jan's appearance—is brief and comes at the very end of the episode, his words are not without impact. "I kind of took a big left turn," he tells Johnson in the scene. "I didn't do a lot of things. I wasn't really thinking. Let me go."

Do you think I wanted my life to turn out this way?

Yes.

His appearance—the trace of charisma between his eyes and jaw, which could still break through his weathered appearance—could've formed the basis for many colorful characterizations, both comedic and dramatic, if only he'd been able to speak more clearly and stand for sustained periods without experiencing stabbing jolts of pain. "The next time I saw Jan, after *Airwolf*, was when he appeared on *The Howard Stern Show*," says Donald Bellisario. "He had that scabby look of an alcoholic, and Howard Stern was telling him how good he looked and how women found him irresistible. I called in to complain about how Howard was exploiting Jan and his alcoholism, and Howard made fun of me."

There were no believers left in Hollywood, but there were still some fans, some of whom had tied their memories of Jan to their childhoods, which they brought to their careers. One of them was filmmaker Steven Soderbergh, who had grown up watching Jan and was, by 1997, looking to move from the art house space he had dominated throughout the decade into the mainstream, a transition that Soderbergh—who later won the Best Director Oscar for the film *Traffic* (2000)—hoped to make with *Out of Sight* (1998), a comedy-crime film, an adaptation of Elmore Leonard's novel of the same name, which starred George Clooney and Jennifer Lopez.

In the summer of 1997, toward the end of the summer, Soderbergh called Jan's manager, Nick Miranda, to inquire about the possibility of giving Jan a role—an unspecified role, as it turned out—in the film. "He [Soderbergh] prefaced his phone call by telling me that, under normal circumstances, he would not even require an audition from Jan but in light of everything he had heard, regrettably, he had no choice," says Miranda. "After the meeting (the audition never occurred), Soderbergh called me, obviously most disappointed. He said he was brokenhearted, not that Jan was unfit to play the part—he was unfit—but by how much he had dissipated from the young virile actor he had become a great fan of."

It is tempting to say that Jan's heartbreakingly funny and sad performance as a broken-down bowling alley manager in the independent comedy-drama film *Buffalo '66* (1998) is his last memorable screen appearance. He hasn't truly acted in nearly forty years.

He retired from acting in 2000, though *White Boy*, an independent film Jan had shot in 1998, was released, unceremoniously, in 2002. Retirement is not something that an actor needs to talk about until they're terminally ill, or they've entered a new occupation. Jan belonged to neither category. "There is little question that, even today, Jan could be a big money earner in his profession had he aged gracefully into the supporting roles that would have still paid him into the millions," says Miranda. "He made a disastrous choice, and he has paid a heavy price. I remember once asking Jan why he drank so much; he looked straight at me and said, 'purely for the kick.' With that, he looked down ruefully at the ground."

His artistic skills, pedestrian as they were, had not been exercised in decades, and his balance was too unsteady for carpentry, the only tradable skill he acquired in all the years he spent in Malibu.

He is still a brother, and an uncle to Christopher and Jacquie's grown children. Amber is married and lives in Portland, Oregon, and the resemblance between Amber and Jan, which was apparent from when Jan held her as a baby, has sharpened over time. He is a non-practicing grandfather.

There is much more money to be made from doing nothing, or next to it, which is not the same as being dead but is chillingly close.

He now receives a full screen actors' guild pension, and there are the residuals from all of the films. This is not an insubstantial amount of money—more than $100,000 per year. It is believed he still holds property in California, in Santa Barbara, but no one is sure—he is no stranger to the IRS, whose collectors have been nipping at his heels for more than a decade, which is one of the reasons he moved to Mississippi. He has sold his story, several times, to the tabloids, and it seems that he will be able to keep doing this for as long as he's alive—the same stories.

Jan with some fans in New Orleans in 2009.
(Photo courtesy of Steve Fenton www.brokentreaty.com)

Lloyd died on August 30, 2000, at the age of eighty, in Hanford, having outlived Doris by more than seven years, which was too much for him. "Because of early childhood issues, Jan was predisposed—without psychiatric or psychological intervention—to turn out exactly the way he has," says Miranda, who holds a Master's degree in psychology. "Lloyd, according to Jan, was a hard, gritty guy, not at all warm and fuzzy."

Jan did jail time in 2000, a first for him, a testament to his lawyers' dexterity and California's overwhelmed criminal justice system, neither of which did him any favors. It was a probation violation, related to the drunk driving and public drunkenness convictions that stemmed from the 1996 crash.

Even the infamous do not receive the same treatment as civilians; Jan's incarceration, in October 2000, took place at the Culver City Police Department, where Jan served as janitor, housed in a special room with a door, not bars. He was permitted visits and the use of a phone; he was denied only satellite television. He emptied trash cans, mopped floors, cleaned the washrooms, and served meals to inmates. He did this for approximately fifty days, quietly and without incident.

Karen Thompson's duties were taken over by Patricia Anna Christ, whom Jan had first met back in the mid-1980s, during the *Airwolf* period, when Jan visited a Los Angeles restaurant that was owned by her ex-husband. She began pursuing Jan in 1998, when she was introduced to him by Jan's manager. "She [Anna] said she'd always been a big fan of his and would love to meet him," recalls Miranda. "She was obnoxious to the point of being overbearing; she asked for Jan's number, and then she asked if I would arrange for her to meet him—she assured me she only wanted to convey her appreciation for his work. I refused. At a point in time, probably to get her off my back, I agreed."

In 2001, Jan declared that Anna—whom Jan was charged with beating up in July 2000—was his third wife. "From the very beginning, he was verbally, then physically, abusive to her in my presence," says Miranda. "He slapped her in the face when she tried to correct something he said. I was stunned and so incensed that I immediately called the police and reported him. I just could not stand by; it was most humiliating, and I could not abide by it—it was a criminal assault. The police came but could not make an arrest, because Anna refused to press charges. In fact, she said no attack had occurred, despite the fact that she had a big bruise across the side of her face—she said she had tripped and fallen against a table. Jan denied striking her; therefore, the police had no choice—they did not arrest Jan. The next day, Anna called and tried to fire me as Jan's manager."

(Photo courtesy of Steve Fenton www.brokentreaty.com)

Anna put up the deposit for the modest house she and Jan shared in Santa Monica in the early 2000s. She paid for the phone and the utilities and provided Jan with whatever money he needed for incidentals, namely cigarettes. She did this by maxing out her American Express credit card, which was eventually refused at a restaurant, which confiscated it.

She took over his life; they moved, on a full-time basis, to Mississippi in 2006, to the remote town of Redwood, where her ex-husband, whom Jan befriended, is from. Jan was in another car crash in 2008, which left him with a broken hip. "I got their number from an ex-boyfriend of hers who is a screenwriter," says Rudy Ramos. "I did call, and he [Jan] answered the phone and was very happy to hear from me. However, someone took the phone away from him and asked who was calling, and then they said to never call there again, and then they hung up. I have had no contact with him since."

In recent years, he has been appearing, with increasing regularity, at the celebrity autograph shows, where his catalog and name value can bring him $10,000, and sometimes more, over the course of a weekend. He receives advance payments from the organizers, so he has nothing to lose.

These shows cater mostly to the horror and science fiction crowd; Jan is usually positioned, in this asylum, somewhere between the genre vanguards—the cult movie stars and scream queens, who have made a second career out of this—and the bottom feeders, whose claim to fame is that they appeared in a single film years ago, which they have extrapolated into a career. They sit at their reduced tables, alone, sometimes for hours, almost begging to be recognized, grateful for the plane ticket, hotel, per diem. Jan is never alone here.

There is a trickle of applause when he is brought out and led to his table, which is outfitted with a credit card swipe machine to make the transactions quick and painless for everyone involved. Then he signs.

More and more, it is the serious collectors, the memorabilia dealers and investors, who crowd him; there is an unspoken understanding that they want his autograph now because they think he's going to die. However, he has been signing so much lately that he has cheapened his brand; the market for his autographed pictures has gone soft, like his belly.

It's time for him to die.

Most biographies begin by asking the same baseline questions: When and where were they born? Who were their parents? What was their childhood like? However, when the end of a subject's life has taken on a life of its own—with a beginning, middle, and an end—two different lives appear, and the beginning of the life becomes the destination rather than a starting point. Everything is upside down.

Let's say he died today, on July 1, 2016. It was almost certainly a heart attack or seizure. It was not sudden; he felt his life being ripped out of his chest, as he was dragged across a garden of fire, God, who is not blameless, wanting him to feel and see everything.

Do you like him?

I don't like myself, which is what we have in common and why I was drawn to him.

Why a book?

That's the most common question they all ask—his classmates, his high school sweetheart, and then his colleagues and friends in Hollywood and Malibu.

"You should search your conscience," his high school sweetheart said to me—this is the same woman who cooperated with that awful *E! True Hollywood Story* special that was done about him. They all still cling to pieces of him.

Do you think this will sell?

I think so. He still has a following, spread across the world, and there have been reappraisals of several of his films. There is his death to look forward to, which will, of course, bring a spike in interest, which will only last a few weeks. This hardly justifies the investment of money and time I've put into him.

That sounds like a hobby.

That is an obsession.

This is only half a book.

This is not a life. It's obvious now that he was not born; he was invented. I thought there would be more, but this is it. He got what he deserved.

How does this end?

I think of that moment near the end of *Big Wednesday*, when Matt Johnson is trapped underwater and is rescued by his friends, one last time, before they let go of him.

Let's say he was alone and drowned. He would like that.

Does it have to be so sad?

I've done my best. He was neither heroic nor sympathetic.

This is goodbye then?

Good night.

Good night, Dark Prince.

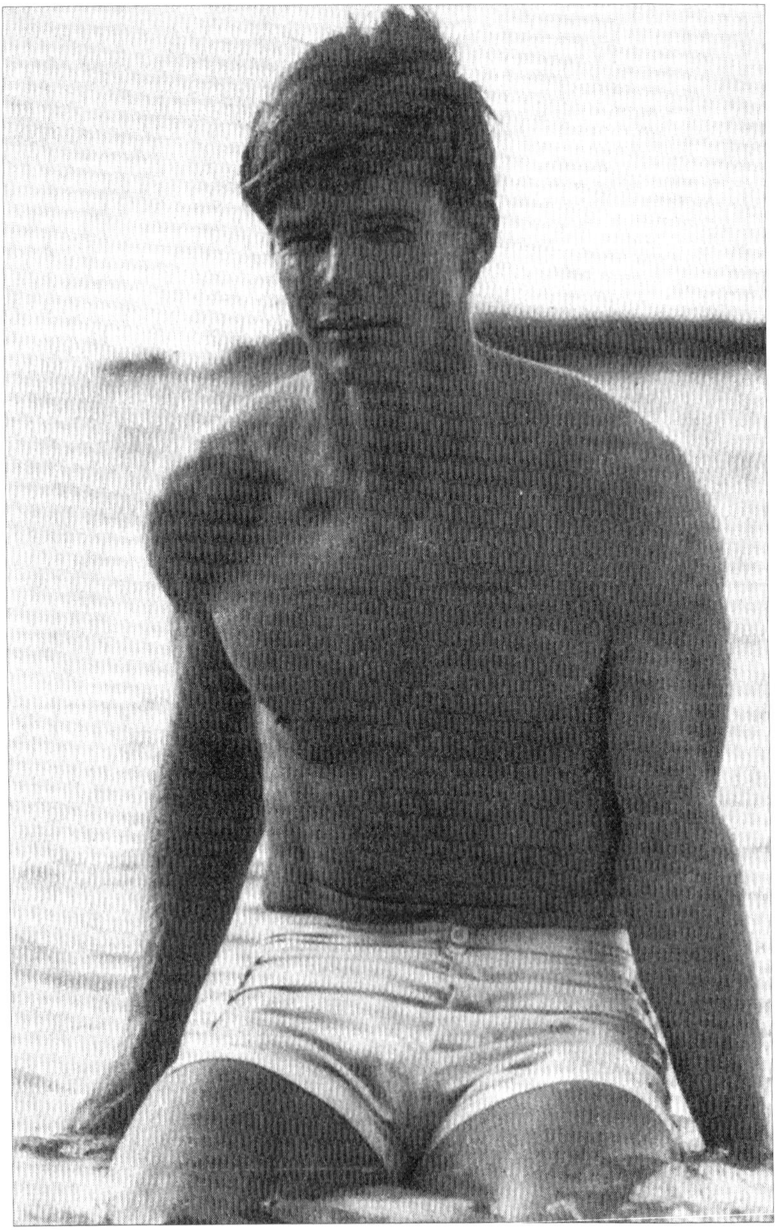

Filmography

Bibliography

Acknowledgments

Index

Filmography (1967–2002)

THE BANDITS (1967; U.S. 1979)

Producciones Zacarias S.A.

Producer: James George. Director: Alfredo Zacarias. Screenplay: Edward DiLorenzo, Alfredo Zacarias. Director of Photographer: Ted Voigtlander. Editors: Gloria Schoemann, Grant K. Smith. Music: Manuel Esperon.

Robert Conrad as Chris Barrett

Manuel Lopez as Valdez

Roy Jenson as Josh Racker

Pedro Armendariz Jr. as Priest

Jan-Michael Vincent as Taye 'Boy' Brown

JOURNEY TO SHILOH (1968)

Universal Pictures

Producer: Howard Christie. Director: William Hale. Screenplay: Heck Allen, Gene Coon. Director of Photography: Enzo A. Martinelli. Editor: Edward W. Williams. Music: David Gates.

James Caan as Buck Burnett

Michael Sarrazin as Miller Nalls

Brenda Scott as Gabrielle DuPrey

Paul Petersen as J.C. Sutton

Jan-Michael Vincent as Little Bit Lucket

THE UNDEFEATED (1969)

20th Century Fox

Producer: Robert L. Jacks. Director: Andrew V. McLaglen. Screenplay: James Lee Barrett. Director of Photography: William H. Clothier. Editor: Robert L. Simpson. Music: Hugo Montenegro.

John Wayne as Colonel John Henry Thomas

Rock Hudson as Colonel James Langdon

Antonio Aguilar as General Rojas

Roman Gabriel as Blue Boy

Jan-Michael Vincent as Bubba Wilkes

GOING HOME (1971)

Metro-Goldwyn-Mayer

Director/Producer: Herbert B. Leonard. Screenplay: Lawrence B. Marcus. Director of Photography: Fred Jackman Jr. Editor: Sigmund Neufeld Jr. Music: Bill Walker.

Robert Mitchum as Harry Graham

Brenda Vaccaro as Jenny Benson

Jan-Michael Vincent as Jimmy Graham

Jason Bernard as Young Jimmy

Sally Kirkland as Ann Graham

THE MECHANIC (1972)

United Artists

Producers: Robert Chartoff, Irwin Winkler. Director: Michael Winner. Screenplay: Lewis John Carlino. Director of Photography: Richard H. Kline. Editor: Frederick Wilson. Music: Jerry Fielding.

Charles Bronson as Arthur Bishop

Jan-Michael Vincent as Steve McKenna

Keenan Wynn as Harry McKenna

Jill Ireland as The Girl

Linda Ridgeway as Louise

THE WORLD'S GREATEST ATHLETE (1973)

Walt Disney Productions

Producer: Bill Walsh. Director: Robert Scheerer. Screenplay: Dee Caruso, Gerald Gardner. Director of Photography: Frank Phillips. Editor: Cotton Warburton. Music: Marvin Hamlisch.

Jan-Michael Vincent as Nanu

Tim Conway as Milo

John Amos as Sam Archer

Roscoe Lee Browne as Gazenga

Dayle Haddon as Jane

BUSTER AND BILLIE (1974)

Columbia Pictures

Producer: Ted Mann. Director: Donald Petrie. Screenplay: Ron Turbeville. Director of Photography: Mario Tosi. Editor: Paul LaMastra. Music: Al De Lory.

Jan-Michael Vincent as Buster

Joan Goodfellow as Billie

Pamela Sue Martin as Margie

Clifton James as Jake

Robert Englund as Whitey

BITE THE BULLET (1975)

Columbia Pictures

Director/Producer: Richard Brooks. Screenplay: Richard Brooks. Director of Photography: Harry Stradling, Jr. Editor: George Grenville. Music: Alex North.

Gene Hackman as Sam Clayton

Candice Bergen as Miss Jones

James Coburn as Luke Matthews

Ben Johnson as Mister

Jan-Michael Vincent as Carbo

WHITE LINE FEVER (1975)

Columbia Pictures

Producer: John Kemeny. Director: Jonathan Kaplan. Screenplay: Ken Friedman, Jonathan Kaplan. Director of Photography: Fred Koenekamp. Editor: O. Nicholas Brown. Music: David Nichtern.

Jan-Michael Vincent as Carrol Jo Hummer

Kay Lenz as Jerri

Slim Pickens as Duane

L.Q. Jones as Buck

Don Porter as Cutler

BABY BLUE MARINE (1976)

Columbia Pictures

Producers: Leonard Goldberg, Aaron Spelling. Director: John Hancock. Screenplay: Stanford Whitmore. Director of Photography: Laszlo Kovacs. Editor: Marion Rothman. Music: Fred Karlin.

Jan-Michael Vincent as Marion

Glynnis O'Connor as Rose

Katherine Helmond as Mrs. Hudkins

Dana Elcar as Sheriff Wenzel

Bert Remsen as Mr. Hudkins

SHADOW OF THE HAWK (1976)

Columbia Pictures

Producer: John Kemeny. Director: George McCowan. Screenplay: Norman Thaddeus Vane, Herbert Wright. Director of Photography: John Holbrook. Editor: O. Nicholas Brown. Music: Robert McMullin.

Jan-Michael Vincent as Mike

Marilyn Hassett as Maureen

Chief Dan George as Old Man Hawk

Pia Shandel as Faye

Marianna Jones as Dsonoqua

VIGILANTE FORCE (1976)

United Artists

Producer: Gene Corman. Director/Screenplay: George Armitage. Director of Photography: William Cronjager. Editor: Morton Tubor. Music: Gerald Fried.

Kris Kristofferson as Aaron Arnold

Jan-Michael Vincent as Ben Arnold

Victoria Principal as Linda

Bernadette Peters as Little Dee

Brad Dexter as Mayor Bradford

DAMNATION ALLEY (1977)

20th Century Fox

Producers: Paul Maslansky, Jerome M. Zeitman. Director: Jack Smight. Director of Photography: Harry Stradling, Jr. Editor: Frank J. Urioste. Music: Jerry Goldsmith.

Jan-Michael Vincent as Lt. Jake Tanner

George Peppard as Major Eugene Denton

Dominique Sanda as Janice

Paul Winfield as Keegan

Jackie Earle Haley as Billy

BIG WEDNESDAY (1978)

Warner Bros.

Producer: Buzz Feitshans. Director: John Milius. Screenplay: Dennis Aaberg, John Milius. Director of Photography: Bruce Surtees. Editor: Robert L. Wolfe. Music: Basil Poledouris.

Jan-Michael Vincent as Matt

William Katt as Jack

Gary Busey as Leroy

Patti D'Arbanville as Sally

Lee Purcell as Peggy

HOOPER (1978)

Warner Bros.

Producer: Hank Moonjean. Director: Hal Needham. Screenplay: Bill Kerby, Thomas Rickman. Director of Photography: Bobby Byrne. Editor: Donn Cambern. Music: Bill Justis.

Burt Reynolds as Sonny Hooper

Sally Field as Gwen Doyle

Jan-Michael Vincent as Delmore "Ski" Shidski

Brian Keith as Jocko Doyle

Robert Klein as Roger Deal

DEFIANCE (1980)

American Interntional Pictures

Producers: Jerry Bruckheimer, William S. Gilmore. Director: John Flynn. Screenplay: Thomas Michael Donnelly. Director of Photography: Ric Waite. Editor: David Finfer. Music: Dominic Frontiere, Gerard McMahon.

Jan-Michael Vincent as Tommy

Theresa Saldana as Marsha

Danny Aiello as Carmine

Rudy Ramos as Angel

Art Carney as Abe

THE RETURN (1980)

Greydon Clark

Director/Producer: Greydon Clark. Screenplay: Curtis Burch, Jim Wheat, Ken Wheat. Director of Photography: Daniel Pearl. Editor: Curtis Burch. Music: Dan Wyman.

Jan-Michael Vincent as Wayne

Cybill Shepherd as Jennifer

Martin Landau as Niles Buchanan

Raymond Burr as Dr. Kramer

Neville Brand as Walt

HARD COUNTRY (1981)

Associated Film Distribution

Producers: Mack Bing, David Greene. Director: David Greene. Screenplay: Michael Kane. Director of Photography: Dennis Dalzell. Editor: John A. Martinelli. Music: Jimmie Haskell, Michael Martin Murphey.

Jan-Michael Vincent as Kyle Richardson

Kim Basinger as Jodie

Michael Parks as Royce

Gailard Sartain as Johnny Bob

Daryl Hannah as Loretta

LAST PLANE OUT (1983)

New World Pictures

Producers: Jack Cox, David Nelson. Director: David Nelson. Screenplay: Ernest Tidyman. Director of Photography: Jacques Haitkin. Music: Dennis McCarthy.

Jan-Michael Vincent as Jack Cox

Julie Carmen as Maria Cardena

Mary Crosby as Elizabeth Rush

David Huffman as Jim Conley

Lloyd Battista as Anastasio Somoza Debayle

ENEMY TERRITORY (1987)

Empire Pictures

Producers: Cynthia De Paula, Tim Kincaid. Director: Peter Manoogian. Screenplay: Stuart Kaminsky, Bobby Liddell. Director of Photography: Ernest R. Dickerson. Editor: Peter Teschner. Music: Richard Kosinski, Sam Winans.

Gary Frank as Barry

Ray Parker Jr. as Will

Jan-Michael Vincent as Parker

Frances Foster as Elva Briggs

Tony Todd as The Count

BORN IN EAST L.A. (1987)

Universal Pictures

Producer: Peter MacGregor-Scott. Director/Screenplay: Cheech Marin. Director of Photography: Alex Phillips Jr. Editors: Don Brochu, Stephen Lovejoy, David Newhouse, Mike Sheridan. Music: Lee Holdridge.

Cheech Marin as Rudy

Paul Rodriguez as Javier

Daniel Stern as Jimmy

Kamala Lopez as Dolores

Jan-Michael Vincent as McCalister

HIT LIST (1989)

New Line Cinema

Producer: Paul Hertzberg. Director: William Lustig. Screenplay: Peter Brosnan, John Goff. Director of Photography: Vincent J. Rabe. Editor: David Kern. Music: Garry Schyman.

Jan-Michael Vincent as Jack Collins

Leo Rossi as Jack DeSalvo

Lance Henriksen as Chris Caleek

Charles Napier as Tom Mitchum

Rip Torn as Vic Luca

DIRTY GAMES (1989)

Action International Pictures

Producers: Roy Sargeant, Albie Venter. Director: Gray Hofmeyr. Screenplay: David Gilman, Gray Hofmeyr. Director of Photography: Anthony Busbridge. Editors: Dean Goodhill, Valma Muir, Nena Olwage. Music: John Weddepohl.

Jan-Michael Vincent as Dr. Kepler West

Valentina Vargas as Dr. Nicola Kendra

Ronald France as Maj. Boissiera

Michael McGovern as Erich Van Kleff

Andrew Buckland as Louis Maurette

IN GOLD WE TRUST (1990)

Action International Pictures

Director/Producer: Philip Chalong. Screenplay: Buncherd Dhawee, Tony S. Suvat. Director of Photography: Visidh Santhavee. Editors: Peter Charles, James Ruxin. Music: Hummie Mann.

Jan-Michael Vincent as Oliver Moss

Sam J. Jones as Jeff Slater

Michi McGee as Sal-Kam

Sherrie Rose as Debbie

Robert Cespedes as George

ALIENATOR (1990)

Image Entertainment

Producer: Jeffrey C. Hogue. Director: Fred Olen Ray. Screenplay: Paul Garson. Director of Photography: Gary Graver. Editor: Chris Roth. Music: Chuck Cirino.

Jan-Michael Vincent as Commander

John Phillip Law as Ward Armstrong

Ross Hagen as Kol

Dyana Ortelli as Orrie

Jesse Dabson as Benny

DEATHSTONE (1990)

Fries Distribution

Producers: Anthony I. Ginnane, Andrew Prowse. Director: Andrew Prowse. Screenplay: Frederick Bailey, David Philips, John Trayne. Director of Photography: Kevan Lind. Editor: Michael Thibault. Music: Gary Stockdale.

R. Lee Ermey as Col. Joe Haines

Jan-Michael Vincent as Andy Buck

Nancy Everhard as Sharon Gale

Peter Brown as Admiral

Pat Skipper as Tony McKee

XTRO II: THE SECOND ENCOUNTER (1990)

New Line Cinema

Producers: John A. Curtis, Lloyd A. Simandi. Director: Harry Bromley-Davenport. Screenplay: John A. Curtis, Steven Lister, Robert Smith. Director of Photography: Nathaniel Massey. Editor: Derek Whelan. Music: Bram Farnon, Robert Small.

Jan-Michael Vincent as Dr. Ron Shepherd

Paul Koslo as Dr. Alex Summerfield

Tara Buckman as Dr. Julie Casserly

Jano Frandsen as McShane

Nicholas Lea as Baines

HANGFIRE (1991)

Motion Picture Corporation of America

Producers: Brad Krevoy, Steven Stabler. Director: Peter Maris. Screenplay: Brian D. Jeffries. Director of Photography: Mark Morris. Editors: Peter Maris, Alex Renskoff. Music: Jim Price.

Brad Davis as Sheriff Ike Slayton

Kim Delaney as Maria Montoya Slayton

Ken Foree as Billy

Lee de Broux as Kuttner

Jan-Michael Vincent as Colonel Johnson

RAW NERVE (1991)

Action International Pictures

Producer: Ruta K. Aras. Director: David A. Prior. Screenplay: David A. Prior, Lawrence A. Simeone. Director of Photography: Andrew Parke. Editor: Tony Malanowski. Music: W. Gregory Turner.

Glenn Ford as Captain Gavin

Sandahl Bergman as Captain Freedman

Randall 'Tex' Cobb as Blake Garrett

Traci Lords as Gina Clayton

Jan-Michael Vincent as Lt. Bruce Ellis

BEYOND THE CALL OF DUTY (1992)

Concorde Pictures

Director/Producer: Cirio H. Santiago. Screenplay: R.G. Davis, Beverly Gray, T.C. McKelvey. Director of Photography: Joe Batac. Editors: Julie Janata, Joseph Zucchero. Music: Nonong Buencamino.

Jan-Michael Vincent as Len Jordan

Eb Lottimer as Lt. Sam Henderson

Jillian McWhirter as Mary Jackson

Vic Trevino as Pete Gonzales

James Gregory Paolleli as Dave Thomas

MIDNIGHT WITNESS (1993)

Academy Entertainment

Director/Producer: Peter Foldy. Screenplay: Peter Foldy. Director of Photography: Thomas F. Denove. Editor: Ron Rosen. Music: Graydon Hillock.

Paul Johannson as Paul

Maxwell Caulfield as Garland

Karen Moncrieff as Katy

Mick Murray as Webster

Jan-Michael Vincent as Lance

SINS OF DESIRE (1993)

Cinetel Films

Producer: Linda A. Borgeson. Director: Jim Wynorski. Screenplay: Peter Liapis, Mark McGee. Director of Photography: Zoran Hochstatter. Editor: Nina Gilberti. Music: Chuck Cirino.

Gail Harris as Monica Waldman

Jay Richardson as Dr. Scott Callister

Delia Sheppard as Jessica Callister

Tanya Roberts as Kay Egan

Jan-Michael Vincent as Warren Robillard

HIDDEN OBSESSION (1993)

Broadstar Entertainment

Producers: Tom Bradshaw, David Glasser, Ralph Server, David Wilder. Director: John Stewart. Screenplay: David Reskin. Director of Photography: James Mathers. Music: Richard Glasser.

Jan-Michael Vincent as Ben Scanlon

Heather Thomas as Ellen Carlyle

Nicholas Celozzi as Joey Phillips

David Glasser as Fredricks

Linda Krus as Sandy Barrington

DEADLY HEROES (1993)

21st Century Film Corporation

Producer: Damian Lee. Director: Menahem Golan. Screenplay: Damian Lee, Gregory Lee. Directors of Photography: Avraham Karpick, Yelhiel-Hilik Neeman. Editors: Carolle Alain, Mari Miklos. Music: Lawrence Shragge.

Michael Pare as Brad Cartowski

Claudette Mink as Marcy Cartowski

Jan-Michael Vincent as Cody Grant

Billy Drago as Jose Maria Carlos

Juliano Mer as Antonio Valdez

INDECENT BEHAVIOUR (1993)

Atlantic Group Films

Producer: Michael Cain. Director: Lawrence Lanoff. Screenplay: Rosalind Robinson. Director of Photography: Anthony G. Nanonechnyj. Editor: Tony Miller. Music: Randy Miller.

Shannon Tweed as Dr. Rebecca Mathis

Gary Hudson as Nick Sharkey

Michelle Moffett as Carol Leiter

Lawrence Hilton-Jacobs as Lou Parsons

Jan-Michael Vincent as Tom Mathis

ABDUCTED II: THE REUNION (1995)

Astral Films

Producers: Boon Collins, Richard Goudreau: Director: Boon Collins. Screenplay: Lindsay Bourne, Boon Collins. Director of Photography: Danny Nowak. Editor: Rick Martin. Music: Ronald J. Weiss.

Dan Haggerty as Joe Evans

Jan-Michael Vincent as Brad Allen

Raquel Bianca as Maria Marcolini

Debbie Rochon as Sharon Baker

Donna Jason as Ingrid Weinhard

BODY COUNT (1995)

A-Pix Entertainment

Producers: Simon Tse, Tony Vincent, David Winters. Director: Talun Hsu. Screenplay: Henry Madden. Director of Photography: Blake T. Evans. Editors: Tony Lanza, Steven Nielson. Music: Don Peake.

Robert Davi as Eddie Cook

Steven Bauer as Vinnie Rizzo

Brigitte Nielsen as Sybil

Sonny Chiba as Makato

Jan-Michael Vincent as Detective Reinhart

ICE CREAM MAN (1995)

A-Pix Entertainment

Director/Producer: Paul Norman. Screenplay: Sven Davison, David Dobkin. Director of Photography: Garrett Griffin. Editor: Andre Vaillancourt. Music: Richard Lyons.

Clint Howard as Gregory Tudor

Justin Isfeld as Johnny Spodak

Anndi McAfee as Heather Langley

JoJo Adams as Tuna Cassera

Jan-Michael Vincent as Detective Gifford

BUFFALO '66 (1998)

Lions Gate Films

Producer: Chris Hanley. Director: Vincent Gallo. Screenplay: Alison Bagnall, Vincent Gallo. Director of Photography: Lance Acord. Editor: Curtiss Clayton. Music: Vincent Gallo.

Vincent Gallo as Billy Brown

Christina Ricci as Layla

Ben Gazzara as Jimmy Brown

Mickey Rourke as The Bookie

Jan-Michael Vincent as Sonny

NO REST FOR THE WICKED (1998)

A Plus Entertainment

Producer: William A. Buzick Jr. Director: John Sjogren. Screenplay: William A. Buzick III, Dino Lee Desby, John Sjogren. Directors of Photography: William A. Buzick III, John Sjogren. Editor: Timothy Scott Ralston. Music: Jimmy Lifton, Scott Sturges.

Stefan Lysenko as Father William

Carla Sofia Lescius as Angelica White

Bryan Kent as Michael

Reginald Bernson as Adam Jackson

Jan-Michael Vincent as Sheriff Juan Ramirez

ESCAPE TO GRIZZLY MOUNTAIN (2000)

MGM

Producers: Randall Emmett, George Furla. Director: Anthony Dalensandro. Screenplay: Boon Collins. Director of Photography: Steve Adcock. Editor: Danny Saphire. Music: Amotz Plessner.

Dan Haggerty as Jeremiah

Jan-Michael Vincent as Trapper

Miko Hughes as Jimmy

Cody McMains as Rollie

Ellina McCormick as Linda Dobson

THE THUNDERING 8TH (2000)

Popcorn Pictures

Director/Producer: Donald Borza II. Screenplay: Donald Borza II. Director of Photography: Andrew Parke. Editors: Chris Salay, Christian Stoehr. Music: Alenander Bubenheim.

Donald Borza II as Joe Sarnowski

Ewing Miles Brown as William Howard

Bo Hopkins as Col. Thompson

June Lockhart as Margaret Howard

Jan-Michael Vincent as Capt. Otis Buchwald

WHITE BOY (2002)

Artisan Entertainment

Producers: Abel Ferrara, Spencer Thornton. Director/Screenplay: John Marino. Director of Photography: Lon Magdich. Editors: Shaun Peterson, Alan Roberts.

Johnny Green as Brian Lovero

Alison Lohman as Amy

Allen Garfield as Mr. Rosen

David Proval sa Jim Lovero

Jan-Michael Vincent as Ron Masters

Bibliography

Amory, Cleveland. "The Very Private World of Jan-Michael Vincent." *Pittsburgh Press*, March 9, 1977.

Anderson, George. "Jan-Michael Vincent: *Going Home* With Regrets." *Pittsburgh Post-Gazette*, July 10, 1974.

Atkinson, Steve. "*Airwolf* Star 'Has Two Months to Live.'" *The Mirror*, March 27, 1999.

Baum, Patricia. "Hollywood's Latest Golden Boy Almost Didn't Make It." *Boca Raton News*, October 16, 1977.

Beck, Marilyn. "Vincent comes back to movies." *Star News*, March 3, 1978.

Borgnine, Ernest. *Ernie: The Autobiography*. New York: Citadel Press, 2008.

Chartrand, Harvey F. "John Flynn: Out for Action." *Shock Cinema*, November 2005.

Eubanks, Joyce Rowland. "Miniseries A High In Career Of Actor Jan-Michael Vincent." *Palm Beach Daily News*, February 1, 1983.

Hilton, Pat. "Vincent Loves Being a Grown-Up." *The Spokesman-Review*, December 28, 1983.

McMahon, Tom. "Jan-Michael Vincent: Former beach bum catches a big wave." *The Montreal Gazette*, April 14, 1984.

Miller, Ron. "Jan-Michael Vincent is Running Out Of Chances." *The Ledger*, June 11, 1986.

Pearson, Howard. "Young *Bite the Bullet* actor in demand." *The Deseret News*, July 4, 1975.

Russell, Bruce. "Jan-Michael Vincent Will Play *The World's Greatest Athlete*." *Toledo Blade*, September 3, 1972.

Shapiro, Dana. "Jan-Michael Vincent." *Icon*, May/June 1999.

Thomas, Bob. "Jan-Michael Vincent stars in two movies this summer." *Boca Raton News*, July 30, 1978.

Acknowledgments

I thank Jan-Michael Vincent—though I've never met him and had no contact with him throughout the writing of this book.

Jan's life began in Hanford, California, where I started with this book. I would like to thank the following people who either agreed to be interviewed or provided information that helped me greatly with this section: Leighton Gould, Jeannie Groves, Dean Hale, Bonnie Hearn Hill, Dianne Milliken, Janet Odell, Charles Oncea, Dee Rose, Jon Rose, and Anthony Sweeney.

Then there are Jan's colleagues and friends in Hollywood and Malibu, whom I want to thank for sharing with me their memories of Jan: Dennis Aaberg, Donald P. Bellisario, Lewis John Carlino, Greydon Clark, Alex Cord, Tony Dow, Robert Englund, Peter Foldy, Danny Goldman, Bill Hamilton, John Hancock, Donald Heitzer, Kim Kahana, Jonathan Kaplan, Larry Lyttle, Paul Maslansky, Nick Miranda, Randy Nauert, Paul Petersen, and Rudy Ramos.

I also want to thank the following people for their invaluable assistance: Kemp Aaberg, Nancy Englund, Steve Fenton, Sandra Kahana, Paul Talbot, and especially Rosie Vukelic, whose website—www.janmichaelvincent.org—is the ultimate online Jan-Michael Vincent resource.

Index

Aaberg, Dennis, 123, 126-129, 161, 178
Aidman, Charles, 86
Aiello, Danny, 137
Airwolf (TV show), 5, 87, 123, 144,146, 151-169, 173
American Graffiti, 121
Anderson, Michael, 31
Aubrey, James, 63

Baby Blue Marine, 55, 104-111, 120
Bandits, The, 32-34, 39-40
Basinger, Kim, 139
Bedelia, Bonnie, 42, 74-75
Bellisario, Donald P., 143, 152-160,163-166, 183
Bergen, Candice, 96
Bergen, Polly, 145
Bernardi, Herschel, 75
Big Wednesday, 119-129, 133, 138, 178
Bite the Bullet, 94-98
Black, Robert, 28
Bochner, Hart, 148, 164-165
Bogdanovich, Peter, 92
Boix, Lionel, 26-27
Bonanza (TV show), 42
Borgnine, Ernest, 153-156, 161, 169
Born in East L.A., 170-171
Boxleitner, Bruce, 79
Bridges, Jeff, 77, 91-92, 121-124
Bronson, Charles, 33, 64-69, 94-95
Brooks, Richard, 94-98
Bruckheimer, Jerry, 134

Buddy Holly Story, The, 123
Buffalo '66, 184
Burns, Catherine, 84
Burns, Michael, 40
Burr, Raymond, 142
Busey, Gary, 120-125, 161, 167
Buster and Billie, 55, 77-85, 92, 100, 146

Caan, James, 40
Cage, Nicolas, 131
Cairns, Ian, 125
Carlino, Lewis John, 66-69
Carney, Art, 137
Carradine, David, 167
Carson, Lance, 121-123
Cassidy, David, 53
Chisum, 50, 77
Cimino, Michael, 92
Clark, Greydon, 142
Clayton, Dick, 28-32, 37, 52
Close Encounters of the Third Kind, 121
Coburn, James, 95
Conrad, Robert, 32-34
Cord, Alex, 86-87, 155, 169
Cox, Richard, 77
Crosby, Mary, 113
Cruise, Tom, 131, 163
Cruising, 77, 98
Curtis, Dan, 143-148, 155, 165

Damnation Alley, 65, 112-119, 128, 133, 138
Dan August (TV show), 59

213

Danger Island (TV show), 43-46, 110
Davis, Jim, 86
Dean, James, 28-29
Death Wish, 138
Defiance, 134-138, 141-142
Deliver Us from Evil, 86
De Niro Robert, 105
Deuel, Geoffrey, 50
Devane, William, 143
Dillman, Bradford, 86
Donner, Richard, 45
Dow, Tony, 41-42, 165
Dragnet 1967 (TV show), 41
Dreyfuss, Richard, 59, 93
Duke, Daryl, 113
Dukes, David, 145

Eastwood, Clint, 49-50, 91-92, 95
Eilbacher, Lisa, 145
Ellis, Chenoa, 166
Englund, Robert, 52, 81-84, 163, 172

Faircloth, Daniel, 82, 85
Feithans, Buzz, 123
Field, Sally, 130, 133
Flynn, John, 135
Ford, Harrison, 29, 59, 119
Foster, Ben, 69
Friedkin, William, 77
Front Runner, The, 98-99

George, Chief Dan, 113
Gere, Richard, 106
Going Home, 55, 60-64, 145
Goldberg, Leonard, 105
Goldman, Danny, 56-57, 73
Gonsalves, Frank, 19-20
Goodfellow, Joan, 81-85
Gordon, Lawrence, 94
Graves, Peter, 145
Grease, 128, 140
Greene, David, 139-140

Guber, Peter, 79, 85, 99-100, 104, 108
Gunsmoke (TV show), 59-60

Hackman, Gene, 95
Hamilton, Bill, 120-126
Hancock, John, 105-106
Hannah, Daryl, 111
Hard Country, 111, 134, 139-141
Hard Times, 94
Hardy Boys, The (TV show), 41
Hassett, Marilyn, 113, 168
Hershey, Barbara, 31
Hill, Walter, 94
Hit List, 172
Holliman, Earl, 56
Hooper, 59, 128-135
Hotel (TV show), 168
Houseman, John, 145
Hudson, Rock, 28, 48
Hutton, Timothy, 131

Ireland, Jill, 68

Jagger, Mick, 177
James, Monique, 32, 37
Jaws, 93
Jaws 2, 128
Jeffers, Gigi, 164
Johnson, Ben, 64, 95
Johnson, Don, 182
Jones, Davy, 53
Journey to Shiloh, 38-40

Kahana, Kim, 46, 68-70, 163
Kane, Michael, 134
Kaplan, Jonathan, 99-104, 114, 168-172
Katt, William, 120, 123-126
Kemeny, John, 100, 112
Kennedy, George, 86
Kiley, Richard, 147
Kowalski, Bernard, 166
Kristofferson, Kris, 108-111

Ladd, Alan, Jr., 116
Landau, Martin, 142, 168
Lassie (TV show), 41-42, 165
Last Picture Show, The, 91-92
Last Plane Out, 147
Laws, Sam, 102
Lee, Monty, 19-20
Lenz, Kay, 101-103
Leonard, Herbert B., 62-63
Leonard, Terry, 126
Lopez, Gerry, 133-135
Lucas, George, 121
Lyons, Robert, 68
Lyttle, Larry, 129

MacGraw, Ali, 145-146, 165
Magnum, P.I. (TV show), 91, 152-153, 159
Mann, Ted, 79, 84
Marcus Welby, M.D. (TV show), 76
Marin, Cheech, 170-171, 182
Marvin, Lee, 103, 177
Maslansky, Paul, 116, 119
Matheson, Tim, 41
Maxwell, Bobby Joe, 135
Melville, Sam, 125
McCowan, George, 111-114
McGavin, Darren, 56-57
McLaglen, Andrew V., 49-50
McQueen, Steve, 49-50, 95, 174
Mechanic, The, 64-70, 74, 86, 93, 104
Milius, John, 121-128, 178
Miller, Roger, 139
Milliken, Dianne, 9, 15
Miranda, Nick, 179-182, 186
Mitchum, Robert, 33, 60-63, 144-145, 177
Monroes, The (TV show), 31
Morrissey, Paul, 77
Murphey, Michael, 134
Murphy, Ben, 145

Nash Bridges (TV show), 182
Needham, Hal, 129
Nelson, Willie, 139

Newman, Paul, 98
Nolte, Nick, 161

O'Connor, Glynnis, 107
Odell, Janet, 17-23, 56
Oncea, Charlie, 19-22, 55, 78
Out of Sight, 183

Pacino, Al, 77
Penn, Sean, 131-132
Peppard, George, 116
Perry, Frank, 99
Peters, Bobby, 18
Petersen, Paul, 40
Petrie, Donald, 79, 82-83, 105
Pickens, Slim, 102
Police Story (TV show), 86-87, 94, 134
Pratt, Deborah, 157, 164

Raiders of the Lost Ark, 119
Ramos, Rudy, 137, 173, 180, 187
Return, The, 141-142
Reynolds, Burt, 29, 49, 59, 95, 129, 130-133
Riddle, Jay, 120, 123
Robinson, Joanne (second wife), 151, 161-162, 167, 174
Rondell, Reid, 162-163
Russell, Leon, 139

Saldana, Theresa, 137
Sanda, Dominique, 116-117
Sandcastles, 43, 74-75
Sarrazin, Michael, 40
Saturday Night Fever, 140
Schwarzenegger, Arnold, 131
Scott, Jean, 159, 164
Selleck, Tom, 91, 153
Seymour, Jane, 165
Shadow of the Hawk, 111-114, 138
Shepherd, Cybill, 142
Sherman, Bobby, 53
Smight, Jack, 112, 116-118

Smokey and the Bandit, 130-132
Soderbergh, Steven, 183-184
Spelling, Aaron, 105
Spielberg, Steven, 93, 121
Stallone, Sylvester, 91, 131
Star Wars, 115, 119
Stern, Howard, 183
Stray Cats (play), 21-22, 31
Stroud, Don, 40, 113
Survivors, The (TV show), 50-52

Taylor, James, 139
Thomas, Richard, 105-106
Thompson, Karen, 179-180
Thunderbolt and Lightfoot, 91-93
Thunderheart, 112
Toma (TV show), 86
Townend, Peter, 125
Trafton, George, 123
Travolta, John, 139-140
Tribes, 31, 55-58, 63, 92
Turbeville, Ron, 78
Turner, Lana, 51

Undefeated, The, 48-51
Urban Cowboy, 139-140

Vaccaro, Brenda, 60
Vigilante Force, 94, 108-111
Vincent, Amber (daughter), 84-86, 92-93, 98, 109-110, 119, 126, 146, 167, 181
Vincent, Anna (third wife), 3-4, 186-187
Vincent, Bonnie (first wife), 18, 25-33, 43-48, 52-54, 74-80, 84-86, 93, 108-110, 119, 126, 151
Vincent, Chris (brother), 7-9, 41, 49, 167, 180
Vincent, Doris (mother), 6-7, 10-12, 26, 78, 167, 173
Vincent, Harriet (grandmother), 9
Vincent, Herbert (grandfather), 7-9, 177
Vincent, Jacquie (sister), 7-9, 49
Vincent, Jan-Michael
  abusive behavior of, 4-5, 93, 119-124, 133-135, 151, 161-162, 186

academic performance, 10, 23-26
acting, approach to, 4, 20-22, 28, 37, 49, 55, 92, 96, 100-103
acting career, decision on, 5, 10, 14, 20-33, 55, 136
acting debut, 21-22, 29-34
adolescent years, 7-18
alcoholism, 3-8, 14, 60-61, 72, 76, 86-87, 92-94, 102-104, 116, 119-127, 133-135, 140-146, 151-161, 166-170, 181-184
appearance, 3-7, 10-15, 21-29, 38, 55-59, 62, 69-76, 94, 102, 120, 132, 140, 155, 159, 171-174, 182-183
awards, 31, 63-64, 77, 147
basic characteristics, 3-15, 20-27, 31, 33, 40-49, 55-57, 100-102, 119, 132, 138, 153-154
birth of, 6-7
car accidents, 3, 26, 139, 174, 178-180
childhood, 6-16
as contract actor at Universal, 32-42, 50-52, 86, 152-153
drug use of, 3-5, 60-61, 76, 86-87, 92, 100, 103, 119-120, 123, 133, 138, 141-142, 146, 151, 155-157, 161-170
education, 10-11, 23-24, 28, 136
as a father, 5, 74-80, 84-86, 92, 98, 110, 119-120, 126, 146, 181
father's death, 185
financial state, 3-4, 65, 110-115, 142, 145, 155, 173, 184-188
gay following of, 28-29, 66-67, 77, 98-99
Hanford, life in, 6-23, 41, 55-56, 76-81, 92, 100, 123-125, 136
health problems, 3-4, 146, 174, 178-183
as a husband, 3-5, 25-27, 43-48, 52-54, 70, 74-80, 84, 86, 108-110, 119-120, 126, 151, 161, 167-168, 181
legal troubles, 4-5, 138, 151-152, 158, 166-167, 180
media attention, 3-5, 16, 49, 94, 180

military career, 6-7, 23-31, 42, 55-58, 64, 92, 104-105
misfit identity, 3-6, 10, 16-18, 27, 29, 58, 100, 104, 127
mother's death, 173
school play, role in, 21-22
screen presence, 3-5, 28-29, 37, 100, 102-103, 132
self-destructive impulse, 3-5, 14-16, 68, 119-127, 156, 163, 168-170
small town values of, 6-15, 23, 57, 78-81, 93, 101, 106, 120, 123
surfing, relationship with, 3-5, 18-27, 78-79, 110, 119-129, 133-135, 140
teen idol status, 3-5, 28-29, 53-54, 71-72, 102
television work, 5, 31, 48, 86, 134, 141-148, 151-169
Vincent, Lloyd (father), 6-14, 19, 20-29, 32, 49, 78, 104, 123, 167, 185

Wagner, Robert, 161
Wahl, Ken, 181-182
War and Remembrance (miniseries), 144-148, 164-165
Watson, Charles, 177
Wayne, John, 48-50, 95, 177
Weston, Jack, 86
White Boy, 184
White Line Fever, 55, 61, 99-104, 114, 144
Whitmore, Stanford, 104
Wiatt, Jim, 129, 133-134, 142
The Wind and the Lion, 121
The Winds of War (miniseries), 141-148, 164-165
Willson, Henry, 28-29
Winfield, Paul, 116
Winner, Michael, 65-69
World's Greatest Athlete, The, 70-77, 86, 104, 147

Young, Neil, 177

Printed in Great Britain
by Amazon